Narratives of Hope and Grief in Higher Education

Stephanie Anne Shelton · Nicole Sieben
Editors

Narratives of Hope and Grief in Higher Education

palgrave
macmillan

Editors
Stephanie Anne Shelton
University of Alabama
Tuscaloosa, AL, USA

Nicole Sieben
SUNY Old Westbury
Old Westbury, NY, USA

ISBN 978-3-030-42558-6   ISBN 978-3-030-42556-2   (eBook)
https://doi.org/10.1007/978-3-030-42556-2

Cover illustration: © Alex Linch/shutterstock.com

This Palgrave Macmillan imprint is published by the registered company Springer Nature Switzerland AG
The registered company address is: Gewerbestrasse 11, 6330 Cham, Switzerland

ACKNOWLEDGEMENTS

We thank our families—both personal and professional—for their support in our times of grief, and for the hope that they have helped us to find and celebrate.

We thank Lindy L. Johnson at The College of William & Mary, for being the one who initially introduced us to one another at the first *JoLLE* Conference in Athens, GA. None of us could have imagined how important that moment was or would be.

So much gratitude to Peter Smagorinsky at The University of Georgia, who constantly encouraged us and supported this project. And cared about and for us as people.

We thank sj Miller for mentorship, support, and love throughout and beyond our losses.

We are grateful to Boden Robertson, whose behind-the-scenes work helped to make this book possible.

We profusely thank the authors of this book for their willingness to share such vulnerable parts of themselves, in order to examine the ways that grief and hope shape higher education.

Stephanie thanks Nicole (of course) for her constant support, love, and generosity. Not a single page would exist without her. She is grateful to her colleagues (and #qualleagues) at The University of Alabama, particularly the #UAQUAL Crew. Thank you to Peter Smagorinsky, Meghan E. Barnes, Michelle M. Falter, and Margaret Robbins for driving all the way to the boondocks of Warthen, Georgia to mourn with her, and for all of her UGA and UA academic families for supporting her in invaluable ways. Thank you to the extensive GHP family for their incredible support, particularly to Lisa Shull, Ricky Parmer, and Jobie Johnson. Thank you to Margaret Shelton, and to Carrie and Becky Brown, for helping Stephanie to recall wonderful memories and to find comfort and joy in those shared moments. Thank you, Jasper, for being the best writing support dog on the planet. And, finally, thank you to Mama, Belle, Tray, Laurie, Colin, Declan, and Genevieve for your impossible support and constant hilarity.

Nicole would first like to thank Stephanie for being a caring, supportive, loving friend, and colleague in the quest for hope amidst the grief. This project is beautiful because of you. Thank you to Laurie Mandel, sj Miller, Robert Petrone, Kia Jane Richmond, Sage Rose, and Laraine Wallowitz for showing up during the various stages of my grief and for inviting critical conversation that made a difference in my world as an educator and hopeful human. Thank you to my SUNY colleagues and students who have shared stories of grief and hope along this journey. Thank you to Nicholas Marc for breathing hope anew into my world. Thank you, Mom, Dave, Joanna, Marc Sean, Sean, the Morantes, Siebens, Ryans, and all my dear family and friends who have loved me through every stage of grief and hope they've been witness to. It is because of you that I am. Finally, thank you, Dad and Mommom, for your continued inspiration from beyond. You are with me in all that I am and all that I do. I love you all, eternally.

CONTENTS

NOTES ON CONTRIBUTORS

Crystal L. Beach is a current high school English language arts teacher in Georgia. Her research interests include literacies, identity, multimodalities, and technologies in the English language arts classroom. Currently, she is working on a sports literacy book and continues to publish and present on her literacy research in the U.S. and abroad.

James Burford is a lecturer in Research Education and Development at the La Trobe University Graduate Research School in Melbourne, Australia. James' research field is higher education, with a particular interest in the political transformations occurring within doctoral education and the academic profession and the felt experience of academic work and life. Alongside Emily Henderson, James is an editor of the research blog on academic conferences: *Conference Inference*. James tweets at @jiaburford.

Deanna Day is Associate Professor in the College of Education at Washington State University. Her research interests include children's literature, reader response theory, reading and writing workshop and digital literacy. She is the 2016 Bonnie Campbell Hill National Literacy Leader and is co-editor of the book *Teaching Globally: Reading the World Through Literature*. She is passionate about helping classroom teachers grow in their literacy and/or technology pedagogy. She believes reading specialists and literacy coaches are integral to elementary and middle schools. Deanna teaches in the online reading endorsement program to help classroom teachers become leaders in their schools.

Nicole DuBois-Grabkowitz is a Long Island-based high school English language arts teacher and the writing support specialist for the Teacher Opportunity Corps (TOC) grant program at the SUNY Old Westbury School of Education. Her research explores the intersectionality between social justice, gamification, and pop culture in education. This is her authorial debut. Find her on Twitter: @NovelTeacherND.

Maureen A. Flint is Assistant Professor in Qualitative Research at the University of Georgia, where she teaches courses on qualitative research design and theory. Her scholarship draws from her experience as a college student affairs professional, her work facilitating intergroup dialogues, and her background in the arts. Maureen's research centers methodological and pedagogical questions of social (in)justice, ethics, and representation through the intersections of theory and artful approaches to inquiry. Her work has recently been published in *The Review of Higher Education*, *Journal of College Student Development*, and *Qualitative Inquiry*.

Nneka Greene is a current Ph.D. student at Regent University (Virginia Beach, VA) studying Higher Education Leadership and Management and a Criminal Justice adjunct at Indiana Wesleyan University (Marion, IN) teaching criminal justice courses. Nneka's research schema includes same-race mentoring, diversity, inclusion and INequity in higher education, and increasing Black and Brown students in tech. Nneka recently published her first co-authored piece in the *Journal of Educational Leadership and Policy Studies*. (https://go.southernct.edu/jelps/files/2019-summer/Griffen.pdf).

Angela Kinder Mains is a nonprofit administrator in Illinois. In her current role, she oversees community engagement, homelessness prevention, and youth development programs. Prior to this, Dr. Mains oversaw adult education and family literacy programming for a refugee resettlement agency, and taught EFL courses in Mainland China. Her research interests include autoethnography, transformational learning theory and resiliency.

Shelly Melchior is a Ph.D. student at the University of Alabama studying Instructional Leadership—Social and Cultural Studies. Her research interests include issues of race and class, and their intersections within the K-12 and postsecondary classroom. She is currently working on her dissertation that specifically looks at the experiences of Black male high school graduates and their understanding and articulation of the accomplishment of the high school diploma.

Lucía I. Mock Muñoz de Luna is a doctoral student in the School of Education at the University of North Carolina at Chapel Hill. She works alongside a community school for Syrian and Palestinian youth in Beirut, Lebanon. Her dissertation will be written in partnership with this school, rooted in a commitment to Palestinian and Syrian futures, decolonization, and liberation.

Lyndsey Nunes is the Inclusive Concurrent Enrollment Initiative Program Director at Westfield State University where she also adjuncts in the Education department. Her research topics include the development and enhancement of self-determination skills of students with intellectual disability, inclusive postsecondary education programs, social-emotional well-being and mental health for young adults with intellectual disability, program evaluation, and staff training. She is an active board member on the Council for Exceptional Children—Massachusetts Chapter and the American Foundation for Suicide Prevention—Massachusetts Chapter.

Boden Robertson is a graduate student at the University of Alabama, where he is completing doctoral coursework in educational research, specializing in qualitative research methods. Boden's research focuses on graduate students teaching in a university context and recently co-authored his first publication in *Social Studies Research and Practice*.

Brandon Sams is an assistant professor of English education at Iowa State University, where he teaches undergraduate and graduate courses on young adult literature and English methods. A former high school English teacher, Brandon focuses his research on the potential of critical, aesthetic, and contemplative reading practices to interrupt and renew "schooled" reading practices shaped by the epistemologies of audit culture. His work has recently been published in *English Teaching: Practice and Critique*, *The ALAN Review*, *Changing English*, and *The Journal of Language and Literacy Education*.

Nancy Rankie Shelton conducts research in urban elementary school settings focusing on the ways in which schools prepare literate, participatory citizens. An active member of the National Council of Teachers of English (NCTE) and the Center for Expansion of Language and Thinking (CELT), her most current books are *5-13: A Memoir of Love, Loss and Survival* (2016, Garn Press) which shares the experience of her husband's diagnosis with stage IV cancer and his death (https://www.facebook.com/513amemoir/), and *Literacy Policies and Practices in Conflict: Reclaiming Classrooms in Networked Times* (2015, Routledge) which examines the tensions between federal policy and effective classroom practices.

Stephanie Anne Shelton is Assistant Professor of Qualitative Research in the College of Education at The University of Alabama, and affiliate faculty member in the Department of Gender and Race Studies. Research interests include examining intersections of gender identities, gender expressions, sexualities, race, and class in educational contexts. Publications have appeared in *English Education*, the *International Journal of Qualitative Studies in Education*, *Qualitative Inquiry*, and *Teaching and Teacher Education*. She is also the co-editor of the book *Feminism and Intersectionality in Academia: Women's Narratives and Experiences in Higher Education*. Twitter: @stephshel78.

Nicole Sieben is Assistant Professor of Secondary English Education at the State University of New York College at Old Westbury where she is also the coordinator for the graduate programs in English education. Research focuses are "writing hope" in secondary and postsecondary education, social justice practices, and professional development in K-12 schools. Sieben is author of the book, *Writing Hope Strategies for Writing Success in Secondary Schools: A Strengths-Based Approach to Teaching Writing*, co-editor for a special issue of *English Education* "Designing Professional Development for Equity and Social Justice," and column editor (2018–2020) for *English Journal's* Books-in-Action column, which focuses on texts that cultivate hope in the classroom. Her work has been published in *English Education*, *Teaching and Teacher Education*, *English Journal*, and *English Leadership Quarterly*. Twitter: @Teach4JusticeNS.

Jeff Spanke is a former high school English teacher and current assistant professor of English at Ball State University. He teaches courses in young adult literature, rhetoric, and composition, introduction to English education, and English teaching methods. His current scholarship examines the various social constructions of teachers, students, and learning with a focus on the intersections of resistance and vulnerability in the education process.

Terah J. Stewart is an Assistant Professor of Student Affairs and Higher Education at Iowa State University. His research and writing are focused on people and populations in the margins of the margins. That is, his research focuses on students with multiple minoritized identities, hyper-marginalized identities, and college students with stigmatized identities. He has studied identity-based college student activists, college students engaged in sex work, and fat students on campus. Additionally, he has written about anti-Blackness in the academy, media, pop culture, and art. Methodologically his expertise is in critical, arts-based, and power-conscious approaches to qualitative research.

CHAPTER 1

From Grief Grew Hope, and This Book

Stephanie Anne Shelton and Nicole Sieben

We, the editors, have known one another since 2011. We were fortunate enough to share mutual friends who introduced us and gave us the opportunity to know, learn from, and love one another. Our relationship shifted substantially in 2014. In July, Nicole's world upended when she and her family lost her father, Marc Sieben; four months later, Stephanie's family lost her father, James "Pedro" Shelton. The circumstances were different. Nicole's loss was sudden—the heartbreak made all the more devastating by the shock and confusion. One day he was healthy, making plans for family vacations and setting new career goals, and the next day he was gone, a fatal medical episode ending those plans. Stephanie's father had, over several years, transitioned from ICU to limited independent living to a nursing home—the sorrow tinged with exhaustion and a small sense of release. Our fathers' deaths continue to tug at our hearts and minds, and they brought us closer in ways that were painful but remain important. As

S. A. Shelton (✉)
The University of Alabama, Tuscaloosa, AL, USA
e-mail: sashelton@ua.edu

N. Sieben
SUNY Old Westbury, Old Westbury, NY, USA
e-mail: siebenn@oldwestbury.edu

© The Author(s) 2020
S. A. Shelton and N. Sieben (eds.),
Narratives of Hope and Grief in Higher Education,
https://doi.org/10.1007/978-3-030-42556-2_1

1

we have healed, our friendship has helped us to slowly, cautiously, gently find hope. That hope never replaces the grief, the two often co-exist, but the hope does thread through the sorrow in ways that help us to grow and to consider ways to help others. This book was born from that grief, that hope, and that desire to support others' sorrows.

HIGHER EDUCATION AND GRIEF

We are both academics in tenure-track positions at universities, and we know from experience that higher education is not equipped to support grief. To be clear, we both have had incredible support from colleagues, mentors, and others. Stephanie's dissertation chair, Peter Smagorinsky, drove all the way to a tiny country church in rural Warthen, Georgia to attend her father's funeral, for example. And, Nicole's dissertation committee members, though she had graduated from her doctoral program the year prior to her father's passing, showed up for her in meaningful ways too. As we've both experienced, the people within the institutions are often thoughtfully present for one another during times of loss; however, it is the institutional structure itself that does not seem to allow for space to mourn. Due dates have limited, and sometimes no, flexibility. Conferences carry on whether we are able to present in our sessions or not. Students deserve to learn, though their instructor's tears might prevent teaching. Tenure and promotion responsibilities remain in effect, and the timeline is rarely adapted to provide more time in these instances. However, despite the academy's resistance to providing space and time to simply grieve, various forms of grief are inevitable components of experiencing higher education. Approximately 35–40% of students experience the death of a loved one (Whitfield, 2019), whether significant other, family, or friend, though certainly not all grief is due to a loved one's death. And, as this book emphasizes, grief has many forms. No matter the form, higher education remains aloof and impervious to the hurt.

An element of that detachment is that, within higher education, discussions of and support for grief are severely lacking, or even nonexistent. Numerous "how to" texts advise ways that those in academia might navigate grief (e.g., Peterkin, 2012; Whitfield, 2019; Zakeri, 2019), but their suggestions are largely detached from the realities of higher education. For example, a sweeping "take care of yourself" (Zakeri, 2019, Para. 4) is a sound suggestion, but it elides situations such as academics and students often being geographically far from support systems, or lacking the time to both "lock yourself in a room for the night and cry" *and* meet various career-essential deadlines. Taking time off from classes is often financially impossible for students or faculty, and grief persists long beyond the allotted number of "bereavement days" that HR policies allow. Additionally, though these discussions regularly encourage that those managing grief access campus-based support resources, the fact is those resources vary widely across institutions. Some colleges and universities offer extensive support; some offer none, with a student, for example, "encountering a professor who tells them, in so many words, to suck it up" (Peterkin, 2012, Para. 7). Most fall in the middle, with some, but ultimately insufficient, help.

And, within these inadequate conversations, the focus is consistently on students. There are incredibly few considerations of what grief looks like for and means to faculty or staff. Any discussions centering these individuals typically either consider the ways that supporting students' trauma affects faculty (Kafka, 2019) or focus on the aftermaths of tragedy for a campus, such as an academic's suicide (Pettit, 2019). Much as we discovered in our own experiences, higher education regularly fails to offer sufficient support to grieving students, and it is utterly unprepared and uncertain of how to support faculty and staff members' pain.

This book is an effort to humanize grief experiences within higher education, and in doing so, to consider ways that academia might do more than simply acknowledge or cursorily support grief. And, importantly, these chapters explore possibilities of finding hope in the midst of that heartache. Certainly, navigating grief is inevitable to the human condition, but finding hope while doing so is essential to healing, and to moving forward in meaningful and empowering ways. Each chapter found in this collection explores grief with the effort of finding sources of hope. To be clear, hope is not a panacea. As is often noted regarding grief, there is no single way to grieve; similarly, there is no one way to hope. Hope calls on multiple pathways toward healing, and it activates our motivations to want to heal in the face of hurt, trauma, and loss. Hope also acknowledges that there will be obstacles to healing, that no pathway toward healing is challenge-free, but that the ways in which we navigate those challenges can make all the difference in surviving our losses and ultimately experiencing full lives of meaning and thriving.

In this collection, each author's narrative is a personal journey for them, woven through with threads of grief, and of hope. The purpose is not to provide tidy, happy endings. That is rarely the way that—even with hope—grief works, after all. Instead, the authors examine grief as a reality in higher education and in doing so assert the possibilities of searching for, and at times finding, hope and healing.

The Chapters

As we both worked to recover from our losses of our fathers (and navigate new losses we both experienced during the writing of this book), we noted the absence of open, vulnerable discussions on grief in the academy. The reverberating silence was not, we knew, because either of our experiences was unique; instead, it was because higher education has not afforded individuals spaces or opportunities to openly share and, in doing so, to heal and form communities of understanding and support across academia. Additionally, what few discussions existed were often steeped in the jargon of mental health services rather than in everyday language. In response to the silence and the babble, the authors in this collection write in narratives. The goals are to make their experiences of grief and hope accessible and human. These are not detached and clinical discussions of loss; these are heartfelt stories, full of open, honest explorations of hurt and of efforts to heal. As a collection, our goal is to companion others in the academy during grief and to allow a community of connection and understanding to emerge as a space for hope to grow within.

Part I: Sorrow and Strength Following the Loss of a Loved One

As we noted, this book began as part of our individual and shared efforts to process our grief when we each lost our father. This first section continues that thread. Each author opens their lives and hearts to share the ways that the loss of a loved one shaped their trajectories in higher education. The section opens with doctoral student Shelly Melchior's chapter, "A Qualitative Reckoning." In the chapter, Shelly shares her complex and sometimes broken relationship with her mother, cut short in their efforts to make amends by her mother's cancer diagnosis. An important portion of Shelly's healing came unexpectedly but unquestionably from her qualitative research courses and her efforts to teach undergraduate education students. Terah J. Stewart, now an assistant professor of higher education and student affairs, reflects on the challenges of finishing a doctoral degree while grieving the loss of his mother in "Hard Grief for Hard Love: Writing Through Doctoral Studies and the Loss of My Mother." Through support systems and loving, grieving letters to his mother, he finds moments of hope and celebrates the ways that his successes honor his mother's life and memory.

Deanna Day's "Losing (and Finding) Myself Through Grief" shows the contradictions that are sometimes inherent in moving through grief to hope. While a faculty member, Deanna lost her husband Boyd to brain cancer, and then, because of the trauma of grief, their daughter through the nine-year-old's inability to process her father's death. Rather than being consumed by the sorrow, however, Deanna used her teaching to find purpose and an individual strength that she had not needed before the grief. In doing so, she was better able to support her daughter's efforts at healing, and to find joy that had seemed impossible before. The first section closes with Maureen A. Flint's "Things That Are Good: Tracing Entanglements of Hope." Through images, lists, and memories, Maureen works through the grief of an ended romantic relationship and her mother's death, all while entangling Maureen's current status as a faculty member with earlier moments in her life, through the tangles of hurt, sorrow, and "things that are good."

PART II: NAVIGATING GRIEF AND NARRATING HOPE THROUGH WRITING

As those contributing to this book are academics, it should come as no surprise that writing is a key component of their professional identities—and of their personal experiences with grief. In the first chapter, Angela Kinder Mains uses autoethnography in "The Art of Bereavement: An Autoethnographic Reflection on Transformational Learning Following the Loss of a Spouse." As her husband Jer grew weaker due to an aggressive form of lymphoma, Angela found an unexpected strength to support their children and to keep the family connected. A few years later, autoethnography became critical to Angela's efforts to process the loss and to celebrate her empowerment. James Burford's chapter, "All at Once: Writing Grief" examines the complexity of grief, when moving between continents both for work and to attend his mother's funeral. The chapter uses poetry and narrative vignettes to move through his sadness, to remember his mother, to find hope and a new determination to live.

Boden Robertson embraces Deleuze's theoretical concept of refrain in "The Refrains That Help Me Remember: An Autoethnography of

Grief, Epistemological Crisis, and Discovering Hope Through Theory" to remember his father. Using phrases that his father often repeated to him, Boden uses these refrains to recall the ways that his father always loved and encouraged him, and in doing so finds new hope in these memories. Nancy Rankie Shelton's "I Can't Complain" uses poetry and journal writing to weave together memories that process her grief in losing her husband Jack, while examining the implications of living in a misogynistic society that complicates her grief and denies her equity.

PART III: HUMANIZING GRIEF IN POLITICIZED MOMENTS

As noted earlier, grief is not only borne from losing a loved one. As the final chapter in Part II indicates, sociocultural and political factors often compound with the personal, and necessitate mourning. Globally, there has been an upswing in gun violence, particularly in the United States. The first chapter in this section, by Crystal L. Beach, "I Refuse to Be a Bystander," recounts Crystal's experience as a survivor of the Virginia Tech campus shooting in 2007, and the ways that event and more recent ones have both traumatized and empowered her as an educator. The second chapter, "Misdiagnosing Generational Trauma and Grief: I Am Not Angry; I Am Triggered and Grief Stricken" by Nneka Green, examines the ways that systemic racism is a constant source of grief as she navigates the endless stereotypes associated with being a Black woman. Using a grief framework more commonly associated with loss of a loved one, Nneka shifts her trauma and exhaustion into anti-racism and anti-sexism. The final chapter in this section, by Lucía I. Mock Muñoz de Luna, is an epistolary narrative. Through a letter to her friend Nour, a Pakistani woman who lives and works in a refugee camp in Lebanon, Lucía explores the complexities of loss and despair, including her fear of misunderstanding and misrepresenting Nour, through her efforts to show and share love.

PART IV: FINDING HOPE THROUGH GRIEF AND ITS QUESTIONS

Grief often comes with a sense of finality. Death, loss, and heartbreak feel absolute and never-ending. This section complicates that notion of grief by sharing narratives that come with and as a result of uncertainty and questions. The first chapter, "'Yup, Just Him': Misconceptions and Our

Table for Three" by Jeff Spanke, shares Jeff's and his wife's grief at learning that, after their son is born, they are unable to have more children. Threaded through that sorrow is the constant joy of their healthy one child and the frustration of others' intrusions on and assumptions of their family of three. Brandon Sams' chapter reflects on and questions the grief of estrangement. "Reading, Loving, and Losing My Mother: A Collage of Partial Understanding" uses the graphic novel *Fun Home* and a collage writing approach to explore his own efforts to understand and navigate his sometimes-existent, always-distant relationship with his mother. While there are no easy resolutions, Brandon ends with hope in recalling the ways that his mother, despite their tensions, has been an important part of many beautiful moments in his life.

Lyndsey Nunes' "Love You to pIeCEs" moves through the grief and near-overwhelming questions of a mentee's suicide. Randi's unexpected death continues to prompt questions, confusion, and heartbreak for all who knew and loved her. However, in the constant questions of "Why?" and "What if?" Lyndsey works to find ways to move her grief into hopeful practices that support her current students and that help her to recognize her own resilience. The final chapter, by Nicole DuBois-Grabkowitz, ends the book specifically because of the beauty, joy, and hope that it offers. Through innumerable questions regarding her mother's health, Nicole and her family overcome a myriad of medical crises to find individual and collective agency and meaning—core elements of an empowering and humanizing hope.

OUR HOPE

This book is not about supplying answers, universalizing grief, or insisting on happy or tidy endings. To insist on positivity in the face of tragedy and loss would be insensitive and unrealistic. Instead, this collection acknowledges and emphasizes that grief is complex, varied, and messy. It is a human condition, and tucking it within sterile clinical concepts does not wash away the often-chaotic nature of grief. This book, then, is about humanizing grief, and about highlighting the ways that hope, even in the most impossible moments, threads through grief. That hope is, like grief, different for each person and is sometimes unexpected. It might be found through remembering, writing, raging, protesting, or questioning. It might be found through ways not yet explored or imagined. Sometimes it is the quest for hope that gives access to hopefulness, as hope is so often found in the journey of pursuit, in the pathways of actions taken, in the stillness of mindful moments, in the rhythms of noticing. These narratives aid in providing pathways to noticing, to building community and compassion in the academy, and to building bridges to hope.

No prescription for finding hope exists, and it is often found accidentally in the movements of living. But, it can be obtained intentionally too. This collection acknowledges all of that—the power of spontaneity *and* intentionally, the purpose of the quest *and* the questions, the persistence of the grief *alongside* the healing. These narratives show that experiencing the power, purpose, and persistence can all happen simultaneously or at specifically defined moments in life, and the authors, each in their own way, share why *noticing* is a valuable step in humanizing their processes of grief and hope.

With the unique imprints that hope and grief carry with them, much uncertainty exists. What is certain, though, is that hope is essential to healing and is an active process. Hope shakes, shifts, transforms, and even heals grief. It does not erase grief—to imply that it does would be a false promise—but it helps the traveler in grief to navigate the path with a wider lens of understanding and compassion for the self and others. Hope promises movement through; it is not a stopping point, but rather a springboard for action. We offer this book as both an action of hope and as a means of sharing narratives that activate hope in the midst of grief. The vulnerability in these pages is sometimes painful, sometimes heart wrenching, sometimes overwhelming, but it is also agentive and always, always hopeful.

REFERENCES

Kafka, A. C. (2019). Overburdened mental-health counselors look after students, but who looks after the counselors? *The Chronicle of Higher Education*. Retrieved from https://www-chronicle-com.libdata.lib.ua.edu/article/Overburdened-Mental-Health/247159.

Peterkin, C. (2012). Campuses offer policies and support groups for students facing loss. *The Chronicle of Higher Education*. Retrieved from https://www-chronicle-com.libdata.lib.ua.edu/article/New-Comforts-for-Grieving/134754.

Pettit, E. (2019). A prominent economist's death prompts talk of mental health in the professoriate. *The Chronicle of Higher Education*. Retrieved from https://www-chronicle-com.libdata.lib.ua.edu/article/A-Prominent-Economist-s/245932.

Whitfield, C. T. (2019). *Managing grief while in college.* Retrieved from https://www.affordablecollegesonline.org/college-resource-center/managing-grief/.

Zakeri, L. R. (2019). Students coping with grief & loss at school. *Accredited Schools Online.* Retrieved from https://www.accreditedschoolsonline.org/resources/managing-grief/.

PART I

Sorrow and Strength Following the Loss of a Loved One

CHAPTER 2

A Qualitative Reckoning

Shelly Melchior

Past. Present. Grief. Yearning. Forgiveness. Pain. Rebirth. Renewal. I sat in class attempting to come up with a theoretical framework to fit a case study project, and nothing fit. Twist and turn, I attempted to make the pieces fit, at a time in my life when every single action felt as if born of the same struggle. I tried to forget my grief—to bury it—but it found me. Faulkner found me:

> So it is the old meat after all, no matter how old. Because if memory exists outside of the flesh—it won't be memory—because it won't know what it remembers—so when she became not—then half of memory became not—and if I become not—then all of the remembering will cease to be—Yes, he thought, between grief and nothing I will take grief. (Faulkner, 1939, p. 324)

And from there this journey of love, loss, grief, and qualitative inquiry begins.

S. Melchior (✉)
The University of Alabama, Tuscaloosa, AL, USA
e-mail: semelchior@crimson.ua.edu

S. A. Shelton and N. Sieben (eds.),
Narratives of Hope and Grief in Higher Education,
https://doi.org/10.1007/978-3-030-42556-2_2

Spring Semester, 2017

"The assignment calls for you to complete an oral history interview on the oldest living member of your family, and it must be at least an hour in length." Six of us, all women in various stages of our doctoral programs, silently took that in—one hour. "And I suggest you not put off deciding who you will interview...Transition." As the professor moved on to the rest of the syllabus during the first session of this Qualitative Interviewing class, I found myself doing exactly what the professor recommended we not do—putting off the question of whom I would interview. I had time. There was no rush to decide, especially considering the logistical nightmare this interview would be, since every living relative was at least 14 hours away. Sitting in that classroom—then—I would never have imagined where this space and this assignment would take me, nor what the opening of that space in that particular classroom would both require of me and allow me to do.

BACKGROUND

Nepantla is the Nahuatl word for in-between. This state of being in-flux "signals transition, uncertainty, alarming feelings of loss, pain, ambiguity, and oftentimes despair...a crossroads of sorts, a nexus point, a space/time of paralysis yet rich with transformational potential" (Keating & González-López, 2011, p. 4). This state of transformation and transition are spaces we universally occupy at some point in our lives; more often, multiple times. My own experience within these liminal, transitional states of transformation (Anzaldua & Keating, 2002; Keating & González-López, 2011) happened to coincide with a series of qualitative research (QR) courses I was required to take as part of a Qualitative Research Graduate Certificate Program at a large public university in the Southern United States.

What began as an oral history interview in a Qualitative Interviewing class soon became so much more. It began a journey of loss, process, pain, awakening, and eventual healing that continued over the course of several semesters; several differing assignments; several different events. It is a journey that is unfinished and may never be. While my experience is solitary, it is not in isolation: "We will not know if others' intimate experiences are similar or different until we offer our own stories and pay attention to how others respond, just as we do in everyday life" (Ellis, 1993, p. 725).

Spring Semester, 2017

I interviewed my father. I sat with my prepared interview protocol and recorded his voice, blue-toothed through the speakers of my car. It was nothing like the original assignment. He was not the oldest member of my family. It was not in-person, yet there was no one else I would have chosen. This man. Left at a fruit stand by teenaged parents, whom he never heard from again. Adopted by a local family and raised with love. He never graduated high school and worked his way up to paving roads. A road-paver's daughter. We were not going to tell my mother about the interview. Too often I was the unknowing pawn in a game I did not know how to play; one where points were scored depending on my loyalty to a particular parent. To have asked him and not my mother was akin to a point on his scorecard. It was best left unsaid, and still he told her anyway, and I listened from my side of our 814-mile distance, with tears in my eyes, as he told me a love story that I was not privy to. My entire life had been spent walking on eggshells. My mother was a manic depressive, alcoholic, Valium addict. Their relationship was angry, often hateful, destructive, and violent. Yet, the interview was an ode to my mother and her place in his life.

Nepantla and the Making of Meaning

QR is at its core about the making of meaning. This concept was lost early on as I found myself treading through murky waters filled with subjectivities, reflexivities, theoretical frameworks, and methodologies we string together to achieve a goal, a grade, and a checkmark. The parameters of this oral history interview assignment were clearly laid out, yet I asked permission to *not* interview the oldest member of my family and to do it from a distance. The professor seemed to sense there was more in this request than I could possibly explain; than I even understood myself. They allowed it, with neither of us having any clue of what this assignment would come to mean.

This became my *stop* moment (Fels, 2012). The moment when QR became more about risk than safety; about the researcher as much as the researched. Fels describes a stop moment as one that "arises when we are surprised or awakened to a moment; we become alert to the suspicion that something else, some other way of being in a relationship or in action, is possible" (2012, p. 53). I interviewed my father seeking some kind of understanding. I wanted to understand who this man was who continued to take hit after hit; who worked from sunup to sundown, never knowing what he was leaving or returning to. I gained a semblance of that understanding, yet, it was what I never saw coming, but somehow felt, that would embody the stop.

Spring Semester, 2017

An interview that I initially did not want my mother to know I was doing, and still, she found out anyway. There was always a competition between them. It wasn't stated; it just was. My mom felt like my dad overshadowed anything she tried to do. I wanted to save her from feeling that again. We had talked about how much my dad enjoyed the process. We had planned to do our own interview; an opportunity not for closure, but for acceptance, forgiveness, maybe understanding. And I put it off. She put if off. It could wait for another day, after all.

Shelly: "Well thank you, Momma. Maybe I will interview you next!"

Mom: "Ooh that would be nice too bad about my drinking days. Whew that would be amazing as you know too too well. Love you and am sorry I was such a mess when you were growing up. I can't imagine what a horrible mess and so violent and just not there for you like I should have been. And I am soo soo sorry about that shelly. I am thoroughly ashamed about all that happened in your young life. It's unforgivable. And I am truly truly sorry for my messy life. That would be some story that's for sure. Love love you."

Shelly: "Woman. I love you. No worries. Maybe we could do an interview and you can talk about that and finally forgive yourself. I promise I did long ago. I love you."

Mom: "Oh my gosh shell [Shelly] that would be so so embarrassing that's for sure. You know I act the same way my dad did, and I said I would never do that, and I ended up worse than him. It's so embarrassing and I can't believe I treated everyone so so horrible. I am so so ashamed the embarrassment I caused all of you. I truly am so so sorry. But that really wasn't me that's not my real self I hope you know. And I try very hard to make up for it. It never took my love from you or dad, but I am sure it was questionable that's for sure. How could it not. I forgave my father and never ever brought it up too him again because I know he was in a bad place. So I really am thankful if u really mean it. Thanks so so much shell it means the world to me. Love love you" (Melchior, personal communication, April 8, 2017).

I wasn't ready to interview my mother. To relive our shared history was to make myself vulnerable and exposed, and so I waited to interview my mother; waited for a day that will never come.

I immediately emailed my professor to tell her what had occurred. By this point, she now knew more about who I was and where I came from than some of my closest friends. In the previous semester, a space had been created where I felt safe in exposure. Those raw, skinned areas that had been covered for so long had been exposed, and maybe, for the first time in my life, I felt responsibility. Whereas in the past, I had carried only blame. I had lived my entire life holding my parents an arm's length away, for their love was the kind that burned.

Vulnerable Spaces

Since this interview was going to occur outside of class, the professor met me to help me submit an IRB application so that I could interview my mother. Her willingness to allow me to take risks and to continue to support this emotional risk-taking created a space of vulnerability on both sides—both teacher and learner. I was laying myself bare because to do an oral history interview with my dad, and then my mom, is to hold your place within their narrative. There was no distancing myself from what I was unburying. The professor was tasked with both reading and responding to what she was given. In her willingness to allow me to take risks, she became a part of the narrative.

Fall Semester, 2017

It is the night of our class party. We are all meeting at Chuy's for dinner and birthday cake to celebrate both the end of class and our professor's birthday. It is the conclusion of another QR class, Qualitative Research II; a new group of faces, but the same professor. I am getting ready to walk out the door when I get a call from my dad that my mom has been taken to the hospital. She is incoherent, and they believe she may have had a stroke. I send a quick email to the professor to let her know what is going on and why I will not be there. Before the night is out, I have received an email sending support and love from nearly every member of the class. The professor did not tell them what was going on, only that something was. Another classmate brought me my class certificate and a box signed by all the members of the class holding a slice of birthday cake. At the same time I am attempting to puzzle through all of the news, 14 hours away from my mom and dad, I feel less alone. In all the assignments, the deadlines, the vulnerabilities, and the pedagogies, I had unknowingly become a member of this classroom community of caring that I did not even recognize was forming until I most needed it.

My mother did not have a stroke. She was instead diagnosed with Stage IV Small-Cell Lung Cancer that had spread to her spine, liver, and esophagus. She had no pain previously. She had no symptoms that we would ever have recognized at the time. She had been to the doctor several times for physicals and her blood work showed nothing that would indicate a concern as large as this one. It is incurable, but treatable.

> *Mom*: "Morning shell, hope all is going okay with you how is school going? I dreamed just this morning you had a horse and foal and the mom was hurt. How crazy are dreams. But please don't get a horse. So hope you have a fantastic day. Love and miss you."
> *Shelly*: "So I died in the dream or just fell off a horse? You and your horses."
> *Mom*: "No. For some reason. You. Just had a horse and foal. And the momma had. Something wrong. With. Her. How crazy is that?" (Melchior, personal communication, November 7-8, 2017)

* * *

Navigating Grief and Narrative Inquiry—Remembering the Unremembered

Our class party was scheduled for December 6, 2018. My mom passed away on December 25, 2018. She did not pass from the cancer that would have claimed her. She passed away after acquiring sepsis due to a secondary urinary tract infection that never should have gone undetected. I never got to interview my mother, and I was left with an oral history interview that never happened. As an only child, I was forced to examine our shared history, because as Faulkner wrote: "then half of memory became not—and if I become not—then all of the remembering will cease to be" (1939, p. 324). Rosenwald and Ochberg (1992) reflect that it is how individuals recount their histories—what they emphasize and omit, their stance as protagonists or victims, the relationship the story establishes between the teller and audience—all shape what individuals can claim of their own lives. Personal stories are not merely a way of telling someone (or oneself) about one's life; they are the means by which identities may be fashioned. (Rosenwald & Ochberg, 1992, p. 1)

My mother was gone, yet she remained in me: "we contain the others; the others contain us" in this "unmapped common ground" (Anzaldua & Keating, 2002, p. 570).

Spring Semester, 2018

I am not looking for absolution. I have actually tried to embrace every wave, every tear, every gnashing and wringing of hand and heart. I think acceptance has been my only goal. Acceptance that it was one thing to receive a diagnosis that was fatal, but quite another to die as the result of sitting in a filthy diaper, all because the treatment that was meant to buy you time, actually took all your fighting ability, and you are left with nothing left to give. I never said goodbye because I never anticipated it was goodbye even as riddled with cancer as she was. It is constant, and yet, when it hits me the hardest; those moments when I least expect it and it attempts to knock me to my knees; when I begin to question all that was left unsaid or all I cannot take back and do over, I think of how she died, and anger fills the spaces. (Melchior, personal memo, April 2018)

As I read through these messages, as I remembered, I began to feel we were in each other's way. We spent so much time defending our choices in relation to each other, that we never took the time to appreciate the fact that no matter what happened, we continued to fight, we continued to defend turf that we thought was our own but was decidedly shared. We were in each other's way, and yet we were each other's way. It was what we knew; a dance in slow motion that never really changed over the years; we just got better at it.

Same professor, one more class on the road to the certificate in QR, and a loss so loud it becomes hard to hear anything outside of it. Here, in this room, I had an outlet to explore my grief, through our shared history, a safe place to remember. Grief is a journey without a map. I became a nomadic wanderer journeying through territory for which, though shared, is absolutely my own. Gloria Anzaldua writes that "By redeeming your most painful experiences, you transform them into something valuable, algo para compartir or share with others so they too may be empowered" (Anzaldua, 2002, p. 540).

I spent the months since my mother's passing reading our emails, reading our texts, looking at pictures, listening to stories, and reliving, remembering, regretting. I search for answers in the *how*. I seek to understand how to navigate this journey through grief as I seek to reconstruct a shared history without a shared historian. I seek a better understanding of the process for how we interpret the unremembered. I also seek a greater understanding of how my role as researcher impacts my navigation of a space where I am both researcher and the researched. Our history is shared. She cannot read this to tell me I am wrong or that I misread a situation, a memory, a text, a moment, and with this knowing comes great responsibility to her memory, to our shared history, to the recounting of the unremembered.

Spring Semester, 2018

I am lost because I no longer know who I am if not the daughter who is being failed by her mother. Don't get me wrong. While my dad took the brunt of her physical abuse, I stand bruised in all the hidden places. I keep people at a distance. I don't let a lot of folks in. I have close to no self-confidence. I am tender and a people pleaser. I have allowed myself to get away with being all of these things, because they were the foundation on which I built my adulthood. I have spent a lifetime distancing myself from being like her. What I am learning through this process is that I am my mother's daughter. I walked in her footprints. She had an alcoholic, violent, abusive father. She was dependent on prescription drugs, and later diagnosed with manic depression and anxiety. I am scared to touch a drink or a pill. I have a need to control my environment and for that reason don't let a lot of folks in. I am easily hurt by even the most innocuous criticism. I try to please others before my own self to the detriment of my own mental and physical health. Our paths were different, and yet, after a lifetime of trying to be nothing like my mom, I find that we are so similar, and there is peace in that. It explains so much. (Melchior, personal memo, April 2018)

Laying the Self Bare

I am a narrative ethnographer, sifting through the scattered ruins of our relationship in an attempt to form a picture of who she was and who we were together, and autoethnographer for in the sharing and the retelling and what I choose to share and retell, I am navigating my own memory, my own grief.

It is deeper than that though, allowing me the opportunity to see how the back and forth of time and memory was never in isolation. These past decisions, choices, moments, and memories are like waves crashing against the shore. It sounds trite, but just as the wave returns to where it belongs, it takes with it grains of sand, sediment, and particles. They are mired and mixed up and unable to separate, and this is also true of my own relationship with my mother. Every interaction, every reaction informs who I am even now that she is no longer here. To be honest, it informed every step I took when she was here even as I fought to claim that was not so. It is a strange space to occupy. So much of my life was spent in a chronic state of mistrust and fear. I pushed and shoved away to protect myself, and I now stand on ground that is constantly wavering for nothing has changed, yet everything has changed. My journey is solitary, yet it is not in isolation.

In the Land of the Shadow-Beasts

Fall Semester, 2018

I am in my final class of the QR certificate. We meet at Starbucks to discuss what my final, culminating project on this journey will entail. We talk about the oral history project and its importance in my own academic career. It was in that space, that classroom, that project, that I began to find my own voice. It was then I asked permission to use it. I no longer feel the need to ask permission.

I did an oral history interview with my dad. I was supposed to do an oral history interview with my mom. I lost my mom. And now I have lost my dad. In August 2018, my father was diagnosed with Alzheimer's. He mourns the loss of my mother every day. His home is a shrine to her memory. He can tell you stories of the past in such a way you believe you are right there in the memory beside him. But he cannot remember he just told you that story, so will tell it again. He is the same and not the same. He was here with us for the holidays and every single night was

Christmas Eve, but if you divert him, he can tell you about that Christmas in 1974 when I got the Holly Hobbie oven that was first on my list. This beautiful man is a shadow of his former self, and he is stuck in a perpetual memory loop that allows no joy in the present. This is my culminating project.

"I am an instrument of my inquiry: and the inquiry is inseparable from who I am" (Louis, 1991, p. 365). I was able to interview my father, and I will hold that memory and those words forever. I have saved the voice recording, just as I still save every message he leaves me. He can still tell those same stories, yet, at some point in these last few years, without even realizing it, I said goodbye to my father, as I knew him, for the last time. He is lost in memories that have no room for the creation of new ones.

These spaces/places/people/faces/moments/memories are all a part of the telling. Just as I most lost all that had defined who I was, I found myself in classroom spaces that encouraged the creation of knowledge as I conceived it, rather than as the neoliberal academy states it should be delivered and regurgitated. Had that not occurred, I may not have lasted long enough in the program to write this piece. Anzaldua writes: "a paradox: the knowledge that exposes your fears can also remove them. Seeing through these cracks makes you uncomfortable because it reveals aspects of yourself (shadow-beasts) you don't want to own" (2002, p. 553).

It was in one of these required QR courses that I first encountered the work of Gloria Anzaldua. Throughout this joint qualitative and personal journey, I continuously found myself returning to her work, and I returned again for this, the final culminating project toward the earning of the QR certificate. While I found continued sisterhood, grace, and peace in her work, I also found myself entering a new state of uncertainty; grappling with her work and my own place within it. As a female, White, novice scholar, was I colonizing her theories and twisting them to fit my own version of her narrative? Anzalduan theories are often bound within the very borders she sought to open—Chicana/Queer/Feminist—and these boundaries kept me from writing, from searching, for in those labels I did not find myself.

Except that I did. This suspicion within that I was appropriating words not meant for me came from my own distrust of an academic community so quick to label, bind, and box. It is risky for a novice scholar to use a theory others will challenge is not her own to use, yet to listen to that inner whisper is to ignore the words on the page and the voice that keeps me returning, rereading, revisiting Anzaldua's work. I found myself drawn to Anzalduan theories with a fear of claiming my place within them, and then read a piece that worried that her legacy would be relegated "into a box, labeling her 'Chicana' and/or 'lesbian' and/or 'feminist' and/or 'queer'" leaving future scholars and lay-writers choosing not to "expand their explorations and understandings of her words" (Keating & González-López, 2011, p. 4). I found a space for both exploration and healing within her words. In those rooms, those assignments, these spaces, her words, I found that "the knowledge that exposes your fears can also remove them" (Anzaldua, 2002, p. 553). I have become a cartographer; responsible for mapping my own journey; and in so doing, I found myself.

Spring Semester, 2019

Our vulnerabilities—as students, as researchers, as teachers and learners, as daughters and mothers, and daughters and fathers—these are the spaces of our shared human experience. It cannot be quantified or justified, but it can be remembered and recorded. In spite of all we shared and lived through, in spite of how often life tried to keep us in separate corners, in spite of the slights, the losses, the hurts that remain; this process, these spaces, this journey, have both transformed and empowered who I am as a researcher and a woman.

There is strength in forgiveness, even if it comes again and again and again. There is healing in our stories. There is power in the telling. There is responsibility in the remembering to acknowledge our own role in the making of that shared history. Until then, I remain charged with the duty of remembering and sharing so as to ensure that when I too, am gone, our stories are not.

I never imagined in that first QR class that my writing, my choice of projects, my studies, would follow this trajectory. Yet, I also do not know that I would or could have moved in these directions in any other classroom. In this professor's classroom, throughout a QR certificate trajectory that spanned five shared classes, I found instead someone willing to "participate with students-materials-discourses in creating knowledges and ways of being/doing QR" (Kuby & Christ, 2018, p. 136); a nudge, one that "enacts students/us; provokes risk taking' and inspires different ways of knowing, creating understanding, and meaning making in our everyday lives" (Kuntz & Guyotte, 2018, p. 268).

You realize that 'home' is that bridge, the in-between place of nepantla and constant transition, the most unsafe of all spaces. You remove the old bridge from your back, and though afraid, allow diverse groups to collectively rebuild it, to buttress it with new steel plates, girders, cable bracing, and trusses. (Anzaldua, 2002, p. 574)

This QR certificate trajectory, these courses, allowed me the space to explore, to process, to transition what has easily been some of the most difficult moments of my entire life. The intra-actions within these QR spaces not only offered me theorists to guide me, nor frameworks to support me, colleagues to encourage me, a professor to challenge me, but most importantly, a space where "risking the personal" (Keating & González-López, 2011, p. 2) allowed for the blurring of boundaries, the queering of ideas, and for me, personally, a place to finally raise my voice beyond a whisper.

References

Anzaldua, G. (2002). Now let us shift…the path of conocimiento…inner work, public acts. In G. Anzaldua & A. Keating (Eds.), *This bridge we call home: Radical visions for transformation* (pp. 540–578). New York, NY: Routledge.

Anzaldua, G., & Keating, A. (Eds.). (2002). *This bridge we call home: Radical visions for transformation.* New York, NY: Routledge.

Ellis, C. (1993). "There are survivors": Telling a story of a sudden death. *The Sociological Quarterly, 34*(4), 711–730.

Faulkner, W. (1939). *The wild palms.* New York, NY: Random House.

Fels, L. (2012). Collecting data through performative inquiry: A tug on the sleeve. *Youth Theatre Journal, 26*(1), 50–60.

Keating, A., & González-López, G. (Eds.). (2011). *Bridging: How Gloria Anzaldua's life and work transformed our own.* Austin: University of Texas Press.

Kuby, C. R., & Christ, R. C. (2018). An ethico-onto-epistemological pedagogy of qualitative research: Knowing/being/doing in the neoliberal academy. In V. Bozalek, R. Braidotti, T. Shefer, & M. Zembylas (Eds.), *Socially just pedagogies: Posthumanist, feminist, and materialist perspectives in higher education* (pp. 131–148). London, UK: Bloomsbury Academic.

Kuntz, A., & Guyotte, K. (2018). Becoming openly faithful: Qualitative pedagogy and paradigmatic slippage. *International Review of Qualitative Research, 11*(3), 256–270.

Louis, M. R. (1991). Reflections on an interpretive way of life. In P. J. Frost, L. F. Moore, M. R. Louis, C. C. Lundberg, & J. Martin (Eds.), *Reframing organizational culture* (pp. 361–365). London, UK: Sage.

Rosenwald, G. C., & Ochberg, R. L. (Eds.). (1992). *Storied lives: The cultural politics of self-understanding.* New Haven, CT: Yale University Press.

CHAPTER 3

Hard Grief for Hard Love: Writing Through Doctoral Studies and the Loss of My Mother

Terah J. Stewart

GRIEF IN THE BEGINNING

So much had changed in my life by the time that I returned to Athens, Georgia. I had left my full-time job, moved out of my apartment, departed from my home state, had prepared to start doctoral studies, and sadly, had buried my mother.

> I've made it safely to Athens. Thanks to everyone for everything that you've done for my family and I, during this difficult time. I have intentionally been "away" from social media so that I can grieve and try to heal with my family but also because I'm not sure what to say at the moment. However, like my mother, I seem to express myself best when I write…I think I'll do that soon. (Stewart, 2016a)

I had approximately two weeks before classes began. At one point, I was incredibly excited for all of the new possibilities that doctoral studies

T. J. Stewart (✉)
Iowa State University, Ames, IA, USA
e-mail: terah@iastate.edu

© The Author(s) 2020
S. A. Shelton and N. Sieben (eds.),
Narratives of Hope and Grief in Higher Education,
https://doi.org/10.1007/978-3-030-42556-2_3

27

would bring, but after having just buried my mother, not even two weeks prior, I just felt numb. We each have our ways of dealing with loss, and only those who have lost a mother, particularly one they were close to, can understand the gravity of what it means to lose one unexpectedly. For me, I wanted to find a way to connect to her: her energy, her memories, connect to *something*, but I was unsure of how to do that. I found myself yearning to do something with the confusion and uncertainty—the grief—that I was feeling. The very next day it happened.

> Tried to do some settling in and began to go through some old photos of family. Something told me to turn on the oldies station that I never listen to and the first song that played was ABC by the Jackson 5. The next song was Midnight Train to Georgia. If you knew anything of my mother, she loved both songs immensely. I don't believe in coincidences. I hear you mom, stay with me. Keep watching. (Stewart, 2016b)

Whether those songs were actually my mom trying to connect with me or the happenstance of a really good radio station algorithm, I needed that moment. I needed the hope of that moment. To share it. And more importantly, to have it affirmed by others. That moment began a cycle of writing through my grief as a means of *doing* something with it. Writing as a way to create, to heal, to remember. I wanted so desperately to be free of my grief—instantly, if at all possible. However, it was the sobering words of bell hooks that reminded me, "At times we will all be confronted with suffering, an unexpected illness, *a loss*. That pain will come whether we choose it or not and not one of us can escape it" (hooks, 2000; p. 210; emphasis added). I began to think of my grief as a process, both ongoing and unyielding, that I could perhaps manage and use to learn about myself.

During the beginning of my first fall semester, I began to refine and craft myself as a scholar, researcher, and writer. Writing as a disciplined practice and a constant developing skill is perhaps the cornerstone of what it means to be in academia. To be a demonstrated scholar, the process of being able to communicate with and through words is tantamount. While writing is always something that I enjoyed doing, it is not necessarily something that came easy to me at first. There are few things that can prepare someone for the rigor, exhaustion, and challenge of doctoral education. Little could have ever prepared me for the experience of losing my mother, and absolutely nothing *did* prepare me to navigate and reconcile both simultaneously.

I recall turning in my first major course assignment, a theoretical synthesis essay that I had no clue how to do. I did all that I could, turned it in, and hoped for the best. I received the following feedback from the professor, who also happened to be my dissertation chair,

> Thanks for your work, TJ. While I know you understand the concepts associated with CRT and Intersectionality theory, your grasp of the concepts is not clear in this paper. Generally speaking, I struggled to follow a lot of the paper, especially as it relates to clarity. I made lots of other suggestions throughout and we will be discussing many of these in class because several people are making the same mistakes—they're common "new to academic writing" errors. I'm also happy to have you revise this paper to earn back some of these points. I think these are important skills to develop, so let's keep working on it!

This feedback was not what I was hoping for, and it was clear to me that I was not successfully articulating my feelings. My ideas and writing were hindered because I was grieving and not confronting the grief I had been experiencing. Given that I was asked to write a lot as a doctoral student, I thought that if I could write where I was hurting the most, then a theoretical synthesis would be a breeze by comparison. So I did:

> My mom died. Passed away. Transitioned.
>
> All of these mean essentially the same thing, they all pain me the same way, but the one most difficult to say is that she died. Not only because there is a certain physical finality but also because it doesn't seem natural to me. My mom, my biggest cheerleader, my mom whom—only second to God—loved me more than anyone in the entire world, is not here with me anymore. It has not been long since she transitioned, but it has already felt like an eternity.
>
> I struggle each day trying to stay in one emotion, in one space. I try to stay grateful that I had such a wonderful mom, and thankful that I had her for as long as I did. Then I'm jerked out of that gratitude and into white hot anger. Resentment. At the world, at God. Trying to understand why. Next, I find myself feeling every bit of sadness one can feel. Devastation. I pull over often because it is hard to drive when you're seeing through your tears. It's an unending cycle, really. These moments and emotions come and go. I once heard someone describe it—grief—as feelings coming in

waves. I don't know that I agree with that analogy. Waves are predictable; there is certain rhythmic nature to them that allows you to anticipate when they might come. That hasn't been my experience. The anger, the sadness, the gratitude all seem to come, and leave, when they feel like it. It's tiring.

There are so many things I could say about my mom. She was truly a phenomenal woman, a wonder to behold. She was the epitome of the phrase salt of the earth. My mom wasn't just liked—she was loved. Deeply, endlessly. Especially by her children and grandchildren. She was our matriarch, our leader, our backbone. As my sisters and I sat around her, holding her hands so we could feel the last of her warmth as it left her body, I looked at them, tears wearing out their welcome on my face to remind them:

"Our momma loved us. If didn't nobody love us, I know mommy loved us."

Silence. And Tears.

…

There really isn't anything that will prepare you for writing an obituary for your mom. Picking out a casket for your mom. Bouncing between knowing it all has to get done and pleading with God that soon you might wake up from the nightmare of having to do it.

At that very moment "Bridge Over Troubled Water" by Aretha Franklin started to play in Starbucks, I looked at pictures of young Mommy in her afro. I am comforted in that moment, that she is with me, still. It was a beautiful moment. One I wish I could have bottled up to take with me on the particularly hard days. I smiled really big.

"I hear you mom."

I miss my mom desperately. I yearn to hear her voice, to tell her I love her, to give her the gifts that I had planned for her upcoming birthday. I want for my life to resume some normalcy, and then it dawned on me that it won't. Life will never, ever, be the same again. Life will never quite feel like home again. And I am learning and praying every day to be at peace with that reality. To know that this is my new normal. A life without my mom's physical presence. I carry her with me, in my heart, in my spirit, in the love I have inside me. I know this, but it won't make me miss the kisses and the hugs any less. I am coming to terms with the notion that my new normal will never feel normal. Life without my mom is not supposed to be. I never want it to feel normal because it makes me know how much I loved her.

It makes me sad to know if I have children, they'll not know the joy that was my mom. As I start my journey to get my PhD, it hurts to know Mom won't be with me on graduation day. She won't be here physically to see all the things I might accomplish. In the same breath I am so grateful that

God allowed us to share so much together before she left. The holidays, the laughter, the food, the love.

I am not sure what all of this means. There is so much I want to write about the timeline of things, about my mom, about all I had hoped to do for and with her, but there isn't the time, nor do I have the energy at the moment. But I believe in reflection, because it allows me to make clear the things I have learned and have yet to learn.

I have learned that life is short. When something wants to shake you to your core, let it. Something might be getting loose; something might be getting free.

I have learned that you should always tell the people you love how much you love them, as much as you can. It'll make moments like these a little better knowing that they know.

I have learned that our ability to heal over the loss of a parent is a testament to the ones who raised us. And though I'll heal, I'll never be "over" it.

Mom, Thank you mom for everything. For your patience, for your love. Thank you for giving us your all. For covering us until your last breath. Thank you for being what I needed, when I needed it. Thank you for showing me what it means to love and be loved. Thank you for showing me how to love myself and how others should love me. Thank you for believing in me and trusting in me. Thank you for always reminding me of what matters in life. Thank you. And please forgive me, for all the ways that I may not have told you or shown you just how amazing, wonderful, and magnificently special you are.

You're a wonder to behold and I am forever changed because I had you to call Mom.

Simply put, my mother was too good for this world. She was too good for us. People like my mom don't last very long in a world like ours. They are meant to come, teach us, love us, and leave—to be magic, to be amazing, in a different plane of existence. I take some comfort in knowing that she is resting and hopefully watching me now, and I know we will meet again. But I know that she was too good for this world, and I was lucky to have her. (Stewart, 2016c)

Grief feels like a volcano that slowly builds pressure in your entire being. Grief weighs you down. It makes you tight. In grieving, I've found that the only way I can relieve the pressure is to *do* something with it. To create. To write. It is through the process of creating that I feel like I can alleviate some of the pressure and breathe. Of grief, bell hooks writes,

Just as the dying are often carted off so that the process of dying will be witnessed by only a select few, grieving individuals are encouraged to let themselves go only in private, in appropriate settings away from the rest of us. Sustained grief is particularly disturbing in a culture that offers a quick fix for any pain. Sometimes it amazes me to know intuitively that the grieving are all around us yet we do not see any overt signs of their anguished spirits. We are taught to feel shame about grief that lingers. To cling to grief, to desire its expression, is to be out of sync with modern life, where the hip do not get bogged down in the mourning. (2000; p. 200)

hooks articulates so much of what I was feeling about academia: That it was not a place open or welcoming to grief. Academia is about order and decorum, and while there may be an acknowledgment of grief, prolonged grieving seemed to be especially egregious. There did not seem to be a place for my grieving, but I hoped to find one so that I could do my best and be a good student, researcher, and scholar. After some time, some of the faculty members in my program encouraged me to continue writing and continue sharing. We mutually began to recognize how giving space to the grief began to make a difference in how I was able to show up as a student and scholar. What I found was that my program and community of practice were incredibly affirming to the grief that I experienced immediately after my mother's death, and well beyond into doctoral studies. The recognition of my grief through writings on social media, on my blog, and other mediums was necessary for me to heal and to grow as a scholar. My hope and healing found fertile ground to begin to grow.

HEALING IN THE MIDDLE

In many ways, I have come to think about the process of writing as a spiritual practice and a healing practice. I found that the more that I wrote about the personal, the better writer I became as an academic, and the better I became as a scholarly writer, the more that I understood how woven together the personal and scholarly are for me. I stumbled on a book, *Writing and Being: Embracing Your Life Through Creative Journaling,* that dramatically shifted how writing came to become a site of healing- and hope-generation, which connected to the academic and to the personal. At the onset, author G. Lynn Nelson (2004) instructs how his book should be—and not be—engaged,

This is not a book about writing. This is a book about *people* writing. It is a book about writing as a tool for intellectual, psychological, and spiritual growth. It is about our language and our being and their powerful interconnectedness, which have often been taken away from us without our even knowing what we have lost. This book is about taking back the miraculous gift of our language and using it as an instrument of creation. (p. xi, emphasis added)

Nelson reframed writing as a process and product of a people, of a person. Our ability to write our stories, our scholarship, and our research is directly connected to our being. Often it seems that writing is touted as a purely intellectual exercise, at times a burden—a necessary *evil* to academic realities. While that may be true sometimes, writing is not *only* that. Writing is also an extension of who we are, who we hope to be, and in my case, a tool to reconcile the metaphysical trauma of losing my mom.

As with many difficult life experiences, things often get better with time. For me, they also got better when I would write. In fact, when I found myself encountering difficult milestones in doctoral studies— authoring manuscripts, candidacy exams, dissertation proposals—I could usually move past any given hurdle by taking some time away to connect with my grief and how it was moving and healing. I took cues to assess my grief and healing from any source that precipitated feelings or thoughts about my mother.

As I continue to grieve the loss of my mom, and as of Tuesday my aunt, Viola Davis' words really resonate with me tonight. (Stewart, 2017)

On February 27, 2017 I had the pleasure to watch critically acclaimed actress Viola Davis win her first Academy Award for Best Supporting Actress. I watched with a heavy heart because my aunt had just unexpectedly passed away; seven months after my mother. In her acceptance speech, David said,

You know, there's one place that all the people with the greatest potential are gathered. One place, and that's the graveyard. People ask me all the time, what kind of stories do you want to tell, Viola? And I say, exhume those bodies. Exhume those stories. The stories of the people who dreamed big and never saw those dreams to fruition. People who fell in love and lost. I became an artist—and thank God I did—because we are the only profession that celebrates what it means to live a life. (ABCNews, 2017)

Her words were piercing and filling at the same time. She articulated a resolve that I had been agonizing over as it related to my grief and how to move through it, when sometimes it felt like I was the only one who cared. When class assignments were due, writing deadlines loomed, and work/assistantship duties never quite simmered down, who was stopping to remember the people whom I loved so much? To remember who they were and to celebrate the fact that they lived, that they existed? After Davis' speech, I began to write a letter that I would not finish for another five months,

Dear Mom,

With the heaviest of hearts, still, I write this letter, hoping against hope it gets to you, and that you hear once more just how much we love you. We, your kids, your grandkids, your village. Who by your own admission were your greatest joy in life; your kids, we face each day, now not having our greatest joy in you.

A year ago today, you transitioned, a moment forever etched in our minds and on the cracks of our broken hearts. An indelible moment, an imprint, one we wish we could forget, yet we hold onto the pain of remembering because it was in those final moments that we held you. We cried, around you, clenching for dear life to the warmth of your body, as it slowly escaped into the atmosphere, along with your spirit and along with our hopes and dreams. We hurt in places and ways we never knew we could, and it is in those same places—in the crevices and caverns of our being—the places where you lived, you filled up, they are now empty, deflated. We find ways to prop them up, so we can continue this journey, this path. But they might not ever be truly full as they once were.

I write this letter to tell you although we are bruised, we're trying not to be broken. Yet we stand on the memories and lessons of your laughter and love, and just know we won't soon forget them.

I miss you desperately. Some days I find myself gasping for air because I'm in such deep thought and remembrance of you that I legitimately forget to breathe. I hear your voice from time to time, and your laughter. They're like air to me.

I completed my first year of school, it was hard, but I found a dope community that holds me up, an advisor who offers me so much grace, and a family, who took your lead and continues to root for me as my biggest fans. I've written some dope things and have some cool projects

I'm developing, and I'm finally going to Africa—Ghana, to be precise. I know you'd be happy.

I try to be a fraction of the embodiment of love like you were, and although I'll never come close, I know you'd be happy that I let love lead the way. Singing at your homegoing is still the most difficult thing I have done, and though I have done a little singing since, my love of song has not returned; it eludes me still.

I hope it makes you smile when we all get together; we have found we feel close to you when we are close to each other. And while I am not personally certain what our meeting will look like on the other side of life, I can't wait either way. We still tread water in a sea of grief of missing you. And yet I am so honored to have had you to call my mom. I've always known that we were fortunate to have you, but it was made clear once your physical manifestation became absent just how lucky we were. I was recently asked what my greatest fear was, and quickly, without a thought, I responded that I didn't have one. It was realized when you departed, and as much as it crushes my entire being to admit that, I hold on to the liberation of love that you left us.

Merriam Webster Dictionary (n.d.) reports that there could be as many as 1 million words in the English language, and I would never be able to string any of them together to tell you just how deeply incredible you were as a mother, and as a human being. It gives us great joy to know that the greatest woman we've ever known found her joy, her purpose, and her love, in us. It is our hope that we honor your legacy of love in humanity, and in God. We'll keep you with us forever.

We are loving you endlessly and missing you always. Be sure to save us some room wherever you are; you know there's a lot of us.

Until next time and love always, TJ

After I wrote and shared that letter again, I felt the volcano within temper down. I felt the waters recede, and as a result, I was able to make progress on several milestones. It was in this instance that it was vividly clear that I was being healed by writing, and the healing was making me a better and more whole scholar. As Gu (2018) asserts,

> Healing, in essence, is the process of making sense of the life story and making peace with it; it is the ability to acquire freedom despite one's life experiences; it is to be the author of one's own life story. It is, after all, the very process of writing. (p. 488)

Indeed, the process of writing was helping me make sense and make peace with my grief and to finally give hope a chance to elevate my being.

HOPE AT THE END

bell hooks once wrote that "to be loving is to be open to grief, to be touched by sorrow, even sorrow that is unending" (2000; p 200), a sentiment that those of us who have experienced grief know too well. As I think about navigating grief, I recall a conversation with a dear friend who—trying to encourage me after losing my mother—said that hard grief is the price that you pay for hard love. That dear friend would also go on to pass away during my time as a doctoral student, and it was a reminder that grief is never that far away. But as my dear friend said to me, grief is the price for love; otherwise, how would you know how much the people we grieve meant to us?

As I near the commencement in a few short months I am hopeful. It still pains me to know that my mother will not be with me on that final day, but I know that she would be proud. More importantly, I know that she would be in awe of how I have been able to navigate the pain of missing her and allowing my best to shine through in the places and projects where I spent my time. As difficult as the doctoral process is/was, it pales in comparison with the difficulty of reconciling the loss of my mom. However, the depth and gravity of that loss rendered visible the reality that everything I need to survive the worst parts of life are already inside of me. Including the ability to write.

There are so many people who have had similar experiences of loss during the doctoral process, which is unsurprising given that life does not stop just because we are doctoral students. I have friends and colleagues who have lost their mentors, friends, and like me, a parent. I hope that this text crosses the path of anyone who may need it. It is a narrative and story that I wish I had had as I navigated the process of grief and doctoral study. I wrote earlier that life after my loss was a "new normal," and I can admit that while I do not care for my new normal, I am—very—slowly learning to function in it. After a recent birthday, I reflected on my life and wrote,

> I miss mom on birthdays more than most days because she *birthed* me. She is the reason I am here, why I am who I am, why I love the way I do. I often concentrate *real* hard and try to imagine what she would

say—maybe not in her exact words—but what would be the essence of her offering to me on today, my birthday? I wonder what she would say if I asked her how to show the universe how grateful you are for another year, and I think Mom would say to just…**live**—live the best life I can. To live authentically, to love freely. She would say to put God first, and I can never lose. She would tell me to keep writing and always believe the best is yet to come. I think she would want me to realize that life is happening, right now…and it's up to me to make it amazing.

And I plan to do just that.

References

ABCNews. (2017, February 26). *Viola Davis oscars acceptance speech for 'Fences' Oscars 2017* [Video file]. Retrieved from https://www.youtube.com/watch? v=YHTXbGG68T8.

Gu, Y. (2018). Narrative, life writing, and healing: The therapeutic functions of storytelling. *Neohelicon: Acta Comparationis Litterarum Universarum, 45*(2), 479–489.

hooks, b. (2000). *All about love: New visions.* New York, NY: Harper Collins.

Merriam-Webster. (n.d.). *Help: How many words are there in English?* Retrieved from   https://www.merriam-webster.com/help/faq-how-many-english-words.

Nelson, G. L. (2004). *Writing and being: Taking back our loves through the power of language.* Novato, CA: New World Library.

Stewart, T. J. (2016a, August 2). *I've made it safely to Athens. Thanks to everyone for everything that you've done for my family and I, during this difficult time. I have intentionally been "away" from social media so that I can grieve and try to heal* [Facebook status update]. Retrieved from https://www.facebook.com/search/top/?q=tj%20stewart%20safely%20to%20athens&epa=SEARCH_BOX.

Stewart, T. J. (2016b, August 3). *Tried to do some settling in and began to go through some old photos of my family. Something told me to turn on the oldies station that I never listen to and the first song that played was ABC by* [Facebook status update]. Retrieved from https://www.facebook.com/search/top/?q=tj%20stewart%20immensely&epa=SEARCH_BOX.

Stewart, T. J. (2016c, August 14). *Anna.* Retrieved from https://medium.com/@TerahJay/anna-8d87da53195d.

Stewart, T. J. (2017, February 26). *As I continue to grieve the loss of my mom, and as of Tuesday my aunt, Viola Davis' words really resonate with me on tonight* [Tweet]. Retrieved from https://twitter.com/TerahJay/status/836086488433582080?s=20.

CHAPTER 4

Losing (and Finding) Myself Through Grief

Deanna Day

Almost three years ago I lost my husband and daughter on the same day. My husband died from brain cancer, and our nine-year-old daughter, traumatized from being adopted and losing two dads, became violent, aggressive, and abusive. Completely weighed down with confusion and grief, I put my academic career on pause and my role as a mother on hold. I was ensnared in trauma. Slowly, through the misery of being without my partner of 17 years and feeling utterly alone, small flickers of hope began to brighten the fog. This chapter shares my journey and the ways that I learned to hold on to hope as I experienced devastating loss.

CANCER JOURNEY

For some individuals, loss and grief come quickly with an unexpected death, but that wasn't the case for me. Cancer can be particularly cruel: shocking at the outset and then offering glimmers of hope before snatching those away. In my case, I began grieving the loss of my husband, Boyd, on the day that he was diagnosed with glioblastoma multiform

D. Day (✉)
Washington State University, Vancouver, WA, USA
e-mail: dday-wiff@wsu.edu

S. A. Shelton and N. Sieben (eds.),
Narratives of Hope and Grief in Higher Education,
https://doi.org/10.1007/978-3-030-42556-2_4

brain cancer. The emergency room doctor showed us a CT scan with an aggressive tumor the size of three golf balls growing on the left side of his brain. Our daughter, who was six at the time, was on my lap reading books. We sat there, stunned and speechless. Soon Boyd was transferred to a brain center where a neurosurgeon scheduled surgery.

This devastating news changed our lives. We were immediately transported into the fast-pace strain of cancer treatments. A month later, Boyd completed six weeks of radiation and daily chemotherapy. Every doctor we saw gave him 13 months to live, yet we were determined to hope for more time. In fact, we displayed the word "hope" in our entryway; it even became part of our computer passwords, reminding us to not give up. And we began praying for a miracle. Hoping the doctors were wrong. Hoping for more time together. Hoping that we would wake up and the cancer would be gone.

The anticipation of Boyd's death caused us to live differently. He made 13 goals for each month he presumably had left. The disagreements couples typically have became trivial. Enjoying these last few months together was all that mattered. He continued taking oral chemotherapy every month, draining his energy, stamina, and desire to eat. Amazingly, Boyd returned to work a year later, which brought some normalcy to our lives. We kept yearning for more months together as he outlived his prognosis. We dared to hope that he might beat this thing.

From the beginning, Boyd was upfront and honest with our daughter, letting her know that someday he would die and go live in heaven. We noticed her stress responses, fight-flight-or-freeze, happened often as she observed Boyd's ongoing doctor visits, weekly blood tests, and numerous MRIs. In her last month of first grade, she stole my cell phone and took it to school, cut a swatch of her hair off, hoarded food from the cafeteria garbage cans, and couldn't complete her schoolwork. A psychologist soon diagnosed her with Reactive Attachment Disorder, because she'd never attached to her birth mother.

During this same period, I was diagnosed with thyroid cancer and my mother with lung cancer. After surgery and treatments, I lived in isolation for over two weeks because I was radioactive. None of us, particularly our daughter, could understand why both parents and her grandmother had cancer. We attended weekly counseling together to build attachment and try to make sense of our lives, but these tragedies triggered multiple emotions in all of us, especially our daughter. Feelings of anger and helplessness permeated our lives despite our best efforts to live each day to the fullest. Still, we clung to hope that all would be well as the days passed, and Boyd lived on.

When Boyd's brain tumor began growing two and a half years later, all of us were plunged into the bleak reality of his terminal diagnosis, entrenched in shock and despair. Our daughter expressed her pain through violence, daily physical assaults on both of us. In addition, she ran away from home, lied about silly things, stole or broke items, and had lengthy daily temper tantrums. When one of these events happened, Boyd's brain would throb, and he had to escape to a dark, quiet room. Boyd deserved to die in peace, so I found a therapeutic home for her to live in as I continued to care for him. At the same time, his mental and physical health made him combative—so angry that he threw things, hurled four-letter words at me, and bawled like an infant when our daughter acted out. Hopelessness flooded our home. I began wondering if any of us would survive.

EMBRACING GRIEF

The end of Boyd's life came quickly and painfully for us. Experiencing the loss of a spouse or partner is overwhelming, the pain excruciating. You are alive, but you don't feel like you are. After Boyd's memorial service, I was left with emptiness and silence. The house was too large, the bed too lonely, and the meals scraped together with little enjoyment. I became depressed, gloomy, and disheartened. Although Boyd was gone, I saw him everywhere and thought of him constantly. I was hurt, helpless, and hopeless. How could this have happened to me, to us?

During the first six months after his death, I was so exhausted from caring for him and managing our home that I slept 12 hours a night. Other comforts included coffee, chocolate, and walking my dogs. I also escaped my pain by streaming Netflix. Some days I was so submerged in sadness that I barely left my bed. I didn't want to live anymore and begged God to take me, so that I could be with Boyd. I agonized over why I was left behind. I rationalized and replayed everything that could have happened differently. Why didn't we go to Duke University and try the experimental drug treatment? Maybe we should have stuck with the ketogenic diet? And sometimes I was in denial that he was even gone.

I soon learned that death and grief are particularly uncomfortable topics for people. I'd experienced death before, after having five miscarriages and losing my grandparents, but until Boyd's death I didn't know what raw, numb pain felt like. Furthermore, I was the first widow in my circles of friends, neighbors, and colleagues and most of them avoided me. They had difficulty meeting my eyes, let alone knowing what to say. Thankfully a handful of friends stayed in contact and walked with me through the ups and downs of grief for the next year.

At this same time, I was engulfed in fear for my daughter. Panic and despair overtook my life. I wondered if she could overcome her anger, become healthy and whole, and if we would ever have the kind of relationship I had dreamed of having with her. She continued to live in the therapeutic home that was three states away, where she refused to do anything: no schoolwork, no chores, and no desire to return home. In fact, she screamed that she hated me. To top it off, my family blamed me for her mental breakdown. Terror suffocated me, and I questioned whether I was losing my mind.

No longer a wife or a mother, I felt misplaced. My faith had been a foundation in my marriage, but I wasn't sure what to believe anymore. I cried my eyes out and demanded, "Why God?" and wondered if I was being punished. A friend suggested that I read a couple of books to give me some encouragement. Guthrie (2002) proposed that I embrace loss and allow grief to work in my life. GriefShare (1998) advised leaning into grief just as one leans into the waves while standing in the ocean. I learned from both of these texts that I needed to travel through my grief, rather than avoid it. It was great advice, but it took a long time before I could follow it.

CHOOSING JOY IN GRIEF

Two months after Boyd's death, a new semester began, and I returned to my university position. I was lonely, depressed, and without desire to teach or write. I wanted to stop brooding and worrying, since these emotions were driving me, but I didn't know how and I wasn't ready. I began isolating myself from friends and couldn't even read children's books, a hobby that I'd enjoyed since childhood. As a literacy and children's literature professor, the thought of reading suddenly made me nauseous. I was confused and frustrated that something that had once provided escape no longer offered solace. Plus, I worried that I would no longer be able to stay current in my field if I wasn't reading.

I decided that I should be honest with my students and let them know that I was hurting. In each of my course syllabi, I explained about Boyd's death and that I was grieving. I communicated that if I seemed emotional, angry, withdrawn, or lonely to not take it personally, because these were parts of grieving. Fortunately, my students were understanding and sympathetic. Teaching gave me purpose and helped me to get up in the morning. Teaching became a joy and pleasure during this very dark time.

Returning to researching and writing was very challenging. In the early months after my loss, I couldn't concentrate. Planning and preparing for classes were difficult. I made many mistakes, had multiple memory lapses with my students, and research and writing suffered. When people asked how I was doing, I pretended that I was okay. It was too difficult to admit that I was overwhelmed with work and grief. After all, how could they possibly understand?

After Boyd's passing, one of his brothers stole his baby album, high school photographs, and army memorabilia. I was so angry that I couldn't talk to him. Family, colleagues, and friends couldn't understand why my daughter wasn't living at home. I felt ashamed and like a horrible mother. In addition, Boyd's parents were having a difficult time processing losing their youngest child and told me that I was no longer family. I realized that these negative thoughts, perceptions, and people were killing any joy that I had. As I deleted my husband's Facebook account, I also deleted my own; social media wasn't bringing me any comfort. Furthermore, I blocked relatives or friends from my phone list who weren't supportive during my grieving process.

The thought of finding joy in the midst of intense brokenness and sorrow seemed impossible, yet I didn't want my loss to be the final chapter in my life. I didn't have the strength to do life on my own, so I poured my heart out to God, asking him for joy. Turning to God comforted and helped me to not be so afraid. I had to trust that he was helping me in my sorrow, even though I didn't see much progress. My faith softened the pain, but it did not take it away.

To combat my stress and fatigue, my doctor had suggested that I join a weekly yoga class when Boyd was diagnosed with cancer. At first I was creaky, clumsy, and uncoordinated, but I made myself return. In fact, a friend picked me up and drove me to yoga twice a week for over two years to make sure that I attended. Holy Yoga eventually became a place of refuge and relaxation as I released my anxieties on the mat. Slowly, I became stronger, steadier, and my stamina grew. The women in this community mourned with me, prayed for me, and loved me. The final relaxation pose during our sessions helped me to release the inner turmoil going on inside my brain, and the tranquil music gave me peace. Holy Yoga truly offered healing, health, and hope for me.

FINDING HOPE IN GRIEF

After Boyd's passing, a hospice chaplain shared the acronym HOPE (Honor, Own, Plan, and Express), which helped me and allowed grief to work in my life. HOPE gave me optimism and options for healing.

Honor *the One You Loved*

I reminisced often with my mother and friends, remembering good memories, creating traditions, and celebrating the time that I had had with my husband. Boyd loved fishing, football, fermented beverages, food, family, friends, and his faith. In his memory, I continued to cheer for the Green Bay Packers and drink his favorite beer. When I went out to breakfast, I ordered his go-to-meal—biscuits and gravy. The chaplain explained that some of my memories might fade over time so I found ways to keep them alive—writing poetry and stories about our travels and his hobbies.

Own *Your Feelings, Don't Hide from Them*

At first I felt lost and abandoned. I cried, whined, screamed, and cried some more. Releasing these feelings helped me to relax. I learned that I had to hurt in order to heal. There was no escaping the pain. In addition, I had to be careful about burying my sorrow in my job. When people asked how I was doing, I eventually learned to be honest and let them know that I was hurting. I stopped pretending that I was okay and began to accept help from friends and neighbors. At first I didn't want to bother anyone, but I came to realize that allowing people to help me let them process their grief, too. One of my neighbors mowed my grass for two years. Another packed up all of Boyd's clothes to donate, and while doing so found Boyd's wedding ring in a jacket pocket.

Plan *Ahead for Holidays, Birthdays, and Anniversaries*

A month after Boyd died, some friends and I celebrated his 55th birthday. A week later, it was our 18th wedding anniversary; a friend and I reminisced about the wonderful marriage we had had together. I took mental health days on these anniversaries and put my classes online so that I could fully attune to my emotions and remember him. The first year, I couldn't go to the beach where we had spent weekends away, but now I visit and celebrate those times.

Express *Your Emotions*

I shared my feelings through journaling, talking with friends, attending a grief support group, and going to counseling. Connecting with others helped me to open my heart and heal from grief. I would have continued to isolate myself, but a friend suggested we meet every Friday for dinner the first year. It was so comforting to have a scheduled time to release my feelings, as she listened and supported me. Writing in a journal helped me to acknowledge and then release my emotions, too. In addition, I attended a 12-week GriefShare (1998) class where I was surrounded by others who'd lost a loved one. The group members understood the different emotions that I was experiencing—from disappointment to bitterness. I also had one-on-one counseling with a therapist, who helped me consider my daughter's trauma.

I've come to realize that my feelings of loss and pain will never leave me, but instead have become part of my story. Nora McInerny (2018) explained that we don't *move on* from grief; instead, we *move forward* with it, because our loved ones will always be present in our lives. There continue to be obstacles in my life, but I am living like there is HOPE, and I am moving forward. I've also learned that by allowing joy and hope in my pain, my heart is slowly healing.

SEEKING GRATITUDE IN GRIEF

Every time I see a family with thriving children and an attentive father, or friends with healthy husbands, I am reminded of my loss. I think, "I should have that" or "That used to be my life." When my envy turned into self-pity and I began avoiding married friends, I realized that I needed to do something about my resentment. I consciously began choosing to live each day looking for beauty and good things. First, I began a gratitude calendar, forcing myself to find something to be grateful for daily. Most days, I wrote my two dogs' names in the calendar squares. No matter how bad a day was, they woke me up each morning to be fed and walked, and their wagging tails made me smile.

Boyd's death and my daughter's absence seemed to dominate my thoughts, controlling some of my emotions and sapping my energy. I didn't want this sadness to define my life. Living with Boyd had been a joy because he had been adventurous, spontaneous, and funny. I began looking for new sources of joy—watching comedy sitcoms that made me belly laugh, joining a K-9 nose class where I trained one of my dogs to identify hidden scents, and continuing Holy Yoga with a supportive community.

Next, I retrained my brain to be grateful as I grieved. For example, when I compound fractured two fingers and required surgery, I added this moment to my gratitude calendar. My throbbing fingers actually caused me to forget my heartache. The laborious exercises and nine months of physical therapy ended up becoming a joy, because they gave me something to do besides focusing on my losses. Switching my brain to focus on the good things helped me to heal.

I also began focusing on the good from my past, remembering God's faithfulness in my life—finding an amazing husband, finishing my dissertation, gaining a faculty position, and becoming a mother. These reminders helped me to notice the good that seemed to be hiding—I was cancer free, teaching was a joy, and I actually enjoyed solitude. I also realized that hating my brother-in-law wasn't helping me heal, even though I thought I'd forgiven him. I gave the issue to God, telling him that I still hurt and asked for a forgiving spirit. Very slowly, over a two-year span, my heart changed toward this brother-in-law.

There is still pain, though. Sometimes things suddenly remind me of Boyd—a steaming cup of black coffee or seeing a Dodge Challenger; these stir beautiful memories and sadness. When a close friend of Boyd's stops by for a visit, floods of memories and tears return. When I walk by a photograph of him, my heart sinks. Boyd loved a certain sushi restaurant, and I still avoid going there. But these setbacks won't last forever.

FINDING PURPOSE IN GRIEF

When dreams have been shattered, it is difficult to find new aspirations and to look forward to the future. My ideal family picture was destroyed when Boyd died and our daughter refused to return home, and new pictures of what a family can be have been very slow to surface. At first I felt like I was no one without Boyd. I'm still trying to figure out who I am and pondering what my next steps are. As I begin another year as a widow, I have intentionally simplified my life, while improving my physical and spiritual selves, and looking for new dreams.

When cancer strikes friends or neighbors, I listen and help them through what was for me a very dark time. Since I know the ins and outs of brain surgery, radiation, and chemotherapy, I suggest questions for their neurosurgeon, radiologist, or oncologist. I have provided text support for families with loved ones diagnosed with cancer. Comforting others who are hurting has given me joy and purpose. Recently, a friend I met at church and I have considered beginning a widows' support group in our community. We both know what it is like to hurt and be hopeless, and we want to be available to and encourage other women. Writing my story for this chapter has also been therapeutic, giving me purpose. Sharing how much I loved Boyd and how grief affected me has helped to release additional emotions. Plus, I hadn't realized I'd found coping mechanisms and sources of joy until I began typing my journey. Although my life with Boyd will always be a part of me, I am becoming a new person and taking risks that I had never dreamed of taking. I'm finding and defining myself anew.

Through losing Boyd, I've surprisingly grown. First, I have learned endurance, patience, and trust—as I have waited for my daughter to heal. I am a much more compassionate person because I know how raw, numb agony feels. I've learned to put my daughter and myself first, versus my university position. I've learned to say "No" and set boundaries. I've let go of perfectionism and am calmer, quieter, and more at ease. I've learned to humble myself and ask others for help—something I never would have done in the past. My heart has changed, leading me to a deeper dependence on God. Lastly, I have immense hope and joy, because I know that someday I will see Boyd in heaven.

Recently, after two and a half years, my daughter returned home. She is 12, and we are in weekly counseling together. I am letting go and leaving her in God's hands; I can't change or fix her, only she and God can do that. Both of us still have immense hurt over Boyd's death and have realized that our lives are going to be different than we had planned. We are working on building and embracing a new future together, looking for purpose and joy when we thought we'd never see it again.

I have been asking for and seeing sparks, joys, passions—new dreams for my life. I honestly have been scared to dream because I still hurt and grieve for Boyd. Furthermore, fulfilling new passions is a lot of work, and it seems easier to stay in the known when life has been so difficult. Yet, I feel called to journey ahead. As a child, I dreamed of becoming an artist, but wondered how I'd pay the bills. This past summer I taught two art classes and rejoiced in the freedom to create and make art all day with my students. Teaching art was like Christmas morning every day. I realized that I'd even teach art for free because I had had so much fun. I feel that I am finally ready to chase lifelong dreams, regardless of what happens.

CONCLUSION

After Boyd died, I was lost, unhappy, and lonely. I had lost my identity and my direction. Plus, becoming a solo mother and supporting a grieving daughter nearly took me over the edge. I'm still working through all of the twists and turns of grief, yet hope continues to surface in surprising moments—watching my daughter bloom and mature, participating in a singles' book club, and returning to watercolor painting after a very long hiatus. I still have a deep wound and several scars, but I keep moving forward. Sometimes I have gloomy days and throw my hands up in the air, but then I see joy in something that changes my spirit. I am not the same person that I was three years ago.

I have come to realize that everyone's grief journey is uniquely their own, and things that worked for me might not work for another. When my mother died two years after Boyd, and then one of my dogs crossed the Rainbow Bridge, these losses triggered deep emotions. I was distressed and discouraged all over again. The ABC's of grief in Fig. 4.1 reminded me to not get stuck in my circumstances. I began journaling again, I returned to counseling, and most of all, I trusted God for help.

Losing a loved one was emotionally, physically, mentally, and spiritually overwhelming. But I have continued to fight, and my heartache has lessened. I've learned to find hope and joy in grief. I will always love and remember Boyd, but I am learning to be brave and embrace new adventures and seek new goals in my life. I continue to press forward. Through endurance, perseverance, and determination, there truly is hope in grief.

Accept what is

Believe in a joyful future

Crying is part of grief

Don't let feelings keep you from moving forward

Express yourself in a journal

Find a grief class or therapist

Gratitude is key to emotional health

Have hope

Isolation won't help

Joy can rise up within you

Keep living your life

Let go of joy killers

Memories won't disappear

Never give up

Overcoming grief is possible

Pain can lead to new passions and purpose

Quit having pity parties, find someone who is worse off and is in need

Remember the blessings of your past

Summon your friends to pray for you

Trust God

Understand the journey may be long

Victory is healing

Worry weakens your spirit

Xtra self-care is necessary

Yesterday is past, find joy in today

Zzzz sleep can help

Fig. 4.1 The ABC's of grief (Adapted from Yohe, personal communication, June 17, 2017)

REFERENCES

GriefShare: Your journey from mourning to joy. (1998). Wake Forest, NC: Church Initiative.

Guthrie, N. (2002). *Holding onto hope.* Carol Stream, IL: Tyndale House.

McInerny, N. (2018). *We don't "move on" from grief. We move forward with it* [Video file]. Retrieved from https://www.ted.com/talks/nora_mcinerny_we_don_t_move_on_from_grief_we_move_forward_.

CHAPTER 5

Things That Are Good: Tracing Entanglements of Hope

Maureen A. Flint

December 1, 2010—12:09 AM

Sophie told me to find paper that felt like home

M. A. Flint (✉)
University of Georgia, Athens, GA, USA
e-mail: maureen.flint@uga.edu

S. A. Shelton and N. Sieben (eds.),
Narratives of Hope and Grief in Higher Education,
https://doi.org/10.1007/978-3-030-42556-2_5

* * *

JUNE 2018

"Find paper that felt like home," I read. My hand brushes the page, cool to the touch, despite the stickiness of the Alabama heat. Crouching over the page, hair pushed back, lips pressed together, I turn the pages. Reading and thumbing through the leaves of cloth-bound diaries, spiraled notebooks, hardcover sketchpads. Sorting through entries that zigzag between times and dates. Tracing nonlinear timelines, remembering as I sit on a hardwood floor with half-packed boxes of books and knickknacks and dishes surrounding me, turning pages. Pulled back to other times and spaces. As the daylight dims around me, I find myself caught up in a then-and-now, resonances and entanglements between the feelings and emotions that the journals mapped, and the present.

* * *

In the pages that follow, I conceptualize hope as working things through, working things out. Hope as working through large and small griefs in granular, minute ways that don't always make sense and are not always linear. Sara Ahmed (2017) wrote that,

> Hope gives us a sense that there is a point to working things out, working things through. Hope does not only or always point towards the future, but carries us through when the terrain is difficult, when the path we follow makes it harder to proceed. Hope is behind us when we have to work for something to be possible. (p. 2)

In this chapter, I travel through time, moving through journal entries compiled and written over the two-year period following my mother's death as I pack boxes, contemplating the ending of a relationship. I travel through time as a working through, as a practice of hope simultaneously behind and ahead, rather than a chronological and linear slicing or segmenting. Specifically, I think time traveling with Barad (2017), who described temporality as "where the 'new' and the 'old' might coexist, where one does not triumph by replacing and overcoming the other" (p. 69). So, as I trace the ridges of tickets and postcards taped and glued, excerpts and annotations from books and movies, along with lists compiled and scrawled late at night, I conceptualize hope as a process of tracing the entanglements between the past and future. Hope as being-there, when being-there is not about pausing time and space, but about affirming entanglements and co-implications with the world becoming, and imagining possible futures. As Barad wrote, "the travel hopper must risk her sense of self, which never will have been one, or itself" (p. 70). Working through, grasping for, desiring possibilities, reconfiguring, reorienting. Hoping.

* * *

I am sitting on the floor, half-full boxes piled around me. Boxes packed to move out of a house that I had longed for, a house that I had walked by countless times over the three years that I had lived in the neighborhood. The house, a two-bedroom bungalow with a rambling yard full of flowers and trees, rose bushes bursting over the walled-in garden in the back. The house pulled me—or I pulled the house, with the stories I told about it— each time I walked by, until suddenly, one day, a for-rent sign appeared in the front yard. I called immediately, seeing that sign, and after a week or two of back and forth, we decided to rent it. And now, just over a year later, I am sitting on the floor of that house, packing boxes to move out. Moving out because the story I had told with that house was entangled with the story of a relationship that had ended.

As I pack up the debris and accumulations of four years, wedging books into boxes, I am paused by the journals that take up the lower shelf of my bookcase. Or perhaps, alternatively, I am pausing with the journals. Lingering. I realize I am holding my breath, taking journals off the shelf one at a time, slowly turning pages. Paging through entries that map the two years following my mom's death. Holding my breath, remembering the period of time when I finished my senior year in college, freelanced and taught and nannied, applied to graduate schools, and eventually, packed up boxes again and moved to Alabama.

* * *

```
ADSTAQ          STAGE 3              ADSTAQ060811E
060811E     NEW WORLD STAGES          925346759341
PROMO       340 WEST 50TH ST, NYC        PROMO
$65.00        AVENUE Q               $65.00
TV          8:00 PM WED              TAVISA TV
060211      JUN 8, 2011
ORCHC       XAWEB1260 0602 B33R          ORCHC
            *INCLUDES $1.50 FACILITY FEE
J  102                              J   102
```

"There's a fine, fine line between reality and pretend" Kate Monster laments in the musical *Avenue Q* (Lopez & Marks, 2003). I had scrawled these same lyrics across a page dated June 8, 2011, a page that also includes the ticket stub from *Avenue Q* that I had attended with Grace, my supervisor at the time. Turning through pages, remembering the mundanity of those two years: to-do lists, ticket stubs from shows and museums, scribbled lines from books, notes from college classes and meetings. Yet threaded through is a refrain that echoes across that time period. Lists that are not to-dos or grocery items or class notes, but instead jumbled compilations of encounters and moments and objects, lists that I had titled "things that are good," or alternately, "things that I know about myself."

* * *

NOVEMBER 18, 2010—11:45 PM

Things that are good:

- The smell of muslin under a hot iron.
- Two eggs over easy, well done hash browns, wheat toast, ice water, and a black coffee.
- Oversized wool sweaters.
- Buying groceries after 1 AM.
- The smell of Play-Doh and
- also crayons.

FEBRUARY 7, 2012

Things that are good:

- Finding new words.
- A full moon hanging in the sky or when the sun makes the buildings look like paper.
- Leftover Chinese food.
- Breakfast for dinner with Grace.
- Instant chocolate pudding.
- Tension tamer tea.
- When Amelia texts me ridiculous things and
- Leah coming to visit me in a few weeks.

* * *

Reading these now, I cannot remember what started them. Maybe it was at the urging of Grace, who supervised me in my on-campus position as an undergraduate Resident Advisor. Grace, who even after I had graduated would invite me over each week to make breakfast for dinner, to watch an episode of *The Good Wife*, to lend me a book. "What good has happened this week?" she would ask me, and I would slowly, reluctantly answer, clasping a cup of tension tamer tea with both hands.

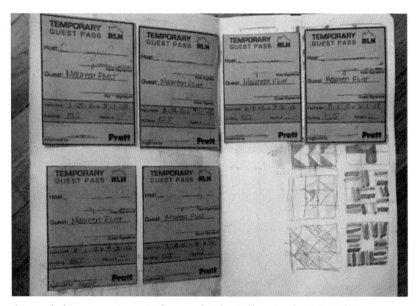

Around the same time, I also read *The Pillow Book of Sei Shōnagon*, a compilation of personal notes, lists, character sketches, and observations made by Sei Shōnagon, a lady-in-waiting to Empress Sadako during the late mid-Heian period in Japan (around 995 AD). I was led to Shōnagon unexpectedly, by another book, a novel called *My Year of Meats* by Ruth Ozeki (1999). Described eclectically on the back cover as "a modern-day take on Upton Sinclair's *The Jungle* for fans of Michael Pollan, Margaret Atwood, and Barbara Kingsolver," what lingered with me from *My Year of Meats* was how Shōnagon's writing guided two of the female protagonists, Jane and Akiko, throughout the novel. Jane cited Shōnagon, "listmaker and leaver of presumptuous scatterings" as her reason for her career as a documentary filmmaker, her inspiration for "to be different" (Ozeki, 1999, p. 15). For Akiko, Shōnagon's lists were a familiar refrain, meditation, and comfort in the face of an abusive relationship, and ultimately, her compass as she started a new life. Ozeki wove excerpts from Shōnagon's diary in the text, including:

101. Squalid Things
The back of a piece of embroidery.
The inside of a cat's ear.

A swarm of mice, who still have no fur, when they come wriggling out of
their nest.
The seams of a fur robe that has not yet been lined.
Darkness in a place that does not give the impression of being very clean.
(Shōnagon, 1991, p. 170)

Squalid things, in particular, stuck with me, enough that I ordered
The Pillow Book, and found myself returning to it long after the details
of Ozeki's novel had faded from memory. Faded, but as Barad (2017)
writes, "the traces always remain" (p. 76), and it was not just *The Pillow
Book,* or Ozeki, or Grace, or the tension tamer tea that led to the writing
of my own lists, but their entanglement. From the possibilities of wriggling mice or the whorls of an ear, to the hopings of Jane and Akiko in
Ozeki's novel, to my own rememberings. "Don't for a minute think that
there are no material effects of yearning and imagining" (Barad, 2017,
p. 78). In each line, each pausing, there are refrains, loops, reconfigur-
ings of hoping, and grieving across temporal and spatial scales.

* * *

JUNE 2018

A journal sitting open on my lap, others strewn around me. I am holding
my breath. The juxtaposition of the ordered and numbered rows and suc-
cinct statements of these lists against other entries, ones that are scrawled
in barely legible script with time stamps of one, two, three in the morning. Moments of grief that surface and repeat over and over across the
pages. Sitting on the floor, I suddenly exhale. Even eight years later, these
feelings still feel too raw to read. And in reading them, the viscerality of
isolation and loneliness, the dizziness of trying to reorient to a world that
has suddenly fallen away is overwhelming. For a moment, time folds and
I am re-feeling these emotions, tears streaming down my face as I sit on
the floor in a house that has grown dark around me. Grieving, holding
my breath.

* * *

May 20, 2010—12:20 AM

almost a month
    it shifts
        not real
sometimes it's real

suddenly this wave of stranded-ness comes over you.
me
it overcame me.

I'm strong
I push through things
I keep going
I'm fine

I want to worry about silly things

* * *

July 19, 2010—8:49 PM

summer in New York is heavy
I've forgotten how to talk to people
I get in these situations and I clam up
Or everything comes out at once
Tripping fumbling
but most of the time I'm silent
        Silent and smirking
            smoking
            smiling
            drinking
it hardly is noticed, my new silence
it feels as though it was always like this
maybe I was

* * *

There is something voyeuristic about grief, even—especially—my own. A fascination or a magnetism to the rawness of it all, the vulnerability, the emotion. And with this voyeurism, grief becomes garish, melodramatic, tawdry. I feel melodramatic at times, writing this. Re-typing the words from these journals into this chapter. As though I am performing for myself, these feelings of grief that are both familiar and distant, immediate and strange. Exaggerated, over dramatic, sensationalized. Do I take a sadistic pleasure in this re-feeling of emotion, poking at the rawness to make sure that I can still feel? Barad (2017) writes that "an embodied practice of re-membering…is not about going back to what was, but rather about the material reconfiguring of spacetimemattering" (p. 63). Dragging myself back through time so that I don't forget—to make sure that I have not. Re-membering, practicing hopefulness that materially reconfigures possibilities for the future, finding possibility to endure.

* * *

January 9, 2012—2:15 AM

I lost my phone again
bathroom at MOMA
someday I'll make a list of it all
the places and ways I've destroyed electronics
I've lost weight
I feel bony, cold
my wrists poke out
ribs
pelvis bones jutting
I don't know when I got like this
I read a book about how the main character became invisible
invisible because no one loved her.
You become visible through the lens of those who love you.
Lately I've felt both visible and invisible.

* * *

Grief, like silence, is often unnoticed. Passed by, unremarked upon, grief can become a way of living and being. Some of that rawness has healed over, even as it is still there, moments of unexplainable loneliness, moments where I discover that I have been holding my breath, following a thought. Remembering. Sitting on the hardwood floor, I am eight years removed, but I still feel the pull of the gaping maw of silence, strandedness, fumbling, invisibility. The yearning, the insistence that I'm fine. I'm fine. I am fine.

As I read through these lists, the sketches, and entries of my grieving, I felt the present moment collapse. Ahmed (2017) writes that "where there is hope, there is difficulty" (p. 2), and I am thinking about the difficulties of these two moments. The ending of a relationship is certainly a different grief than death, but it is an ending. There is something lost. Your world is pulled away, you are suddenly not the person you were before.

* * *

September 8, 2010

Things I like:

- Being barefoot.
- My writing better with black pens.
- Lipstick stains on coffee mugs.
- Pin curls.
- Earl gray tea with milk and sugar.
- Woodsmoke.

* * *

December 7, 2010

Good things:

- Climbing into bed exhausted and feeling your whole body relax.
- Earl gray tea with cream and sugar.
- Windy days with long skirts flying around your legs.
- Black pens.
- Butter pecan ice cream.

- Oldies radio stations.
- Unexpected lipstick.
- Going barefoot.
- Flannel.

* * *

As for Akiko in Ozeki's novel, these lists are comforting in their repetition. Their repetition among themselves, familiar pathways and echoes of earl gray tea with milk and sugar, black pens, lipstick, and being barefoot, as well as their familiarity, re-reading them. A recognition. In the midst of grief, grief that had become part of who I was, these lists work the tension between grief and hope, between the void that echoes in entries written late at night, bleary and numb. Barad (2017) described the void as, "a lively tension that troubles the opposition between living and dying...flush with yearning, with innumerable possibilities/imaginings of what was, could be, might yet have been, all co-existing" (p. 79). The lists, in their repetition and cadence, were not about reinventing who I was or finding new things, but about tracing the lines of the material configurations of which I was a part, yearning for the possibilities that they offered. Of textures and feelings and sounds and relations that are still becoming. These practices "produce openings, new possible histories by which time-beings might find ways to endure" (Barad, 2017, p. 63). Lists, tracing material configurations that are at once comfortable and novel, reasserting being-there in relation with other places and people and things, when they had become in other ways unrecognizable. These lists in their repetition are a hopefulness, remembering, returning, reconfiguring.

* * *

JUNE 30, 2011—6:20 PM

There was this movie I watched last week, *Princess Kaiulani*, she picked up shells, and gave each shell a memory. Carried them around in a velvet bag. (Forby, 2009)

The book I finished *Belong to Me* one of the characters talks about putting all her rage in this ornate box her mother gave her. (Santos, 2011)
I do that, these things together, give objects memories then place them away when I don't want to think about it. Carry them with me even as I put them away.

* * *

OCTOBER 5, 2010—1:37 AM

I don't think my brain has comprehended it yet
    her, gone.
Logically, I know.
But when I actually start to think about it, it doesn't make sense.
So, when I talk about her,
    my head doesn't think she's not here.
Because – something that integral can't just disappear, right?
    It's cold, it rained all day.

* * *

JANUARY 2019

I am talking on the phone, about this chapter, about my apprehension in writing it. I am not sure if I am ready. To write about mom, to write about this other ending. To work through, to think about grief and hope. To re-trace these material configurations, to travel through time. To write about all of this in a way that is not so raw that it becomes unbearable—to myself and to you. I am not sure if I am ready to think with this moment of sitting on the floor. Of the connections between these two encounters of ending and packing up boxes.

* * *

OCTOBER 4, 2010

I have a zit on my cheek.
Also, at the corner of my lip.
I don't know why this seems important, but it does.
I'm ~~desperately~~ trying to focus on something.
    Anything.

* * *

Barad (2017) asked "what does it mean to swallow an event?...to take it into your gut, to feel it leach into your bones, mutate your innards, and reset your cellular clocks?" (p. 81). Sitting on the floor, I think about how I have swallowed—am still swallowing—both of these events, my mother's death and the end of this relationship. The lines that I am drawing between them, these endings, these griefs, are not from an attempt to equate them, or move beyond them. Rather, I am wondering how I have taken—am taking—them inside, how they have made—are making—different configurations and becomings possible. A swallowing that is productive and affirmative. My mom's death was sad, still evokes sadness. I feel lonely without her, like there is something missing that will never be filled. And, in tracing the entanglements of her loss, my grieving, these lists, my hopings, I am returning to her, remembering her effects and modulations in the present. I have become the woman that I am because of her, and even as some of my journal entries are raw and emotional, they mark moments of becoming. Even as at times, re-reading them, I feel not just sadness, but exasperation and embarrassment and frustration with my former self. Trying to capture the excesses produced by grief is a failed project. A failed project that can feel performative and melodramatic. And yet, in their excess, these entries are moments of claiming feelings and emotions. Barad (2017) writes that "what makes us human is...our relationship with and responsibility to the dead, to the ghosts of the past and the future" (p. 87). Practicing responsibility. Working through, wading through these entries, not to find an ending or to get there, but to be in it, the entanglements and relationships of being human. The entries are markers of grieving, and they are markers of hope.

* * *

December 19, 2010

Good things:

- Ivory soap smell.
- Finding a penny on the ground.
- Having the perfect song come on shuffle.
- Coming home to the smell of a woodstove.
- Holiday lights.
- Taking out pin curls.
- When the air smells like snow.
- Winter socks.
- Sequined clothing.
- Rediscovering books from middle school.

* * *

Scrawling journal entries late at night, making lists of good things, then, is a process of claiming, tracing, returning. A process of hoping. Tracing entanglements, even when it is too much or embarrassing in retrospect, or when it hurts to come back to. Especially then. And now, I am thinking about this other ending, the ending of a relationship, as another assertion of being-there, being human. Even as that being-there is disoriented and ruptured, the choice to end something, to move on differently, is a claim on the relationships and responsibilities you want to become with. Another kind of hoping.

* * *

July 12, 2011—12:49 AM

Things that are good:

- Cracking an ice cube tray and having all the cubes come loose.
- Vegetables on sale at the corner store.
- Tan lines on your fingers from rings.
- Tangerine lipstick.
- Frozen whoopie pies from Grace's freezer.

- Blasts of air conditioning as you walk by a store.
- Air conditioning, period.
- Crimps in your hair from a braid.
- Washing your face after being outside on a hot, sticky day.
- Long skirts and bikes.
- Long skirts, sandals, and bikes.
- Plans.

* * *

February 2019

I am sitting on the hard wooden bench of a coffee shop, a cappuccino that has become cold sitting next to me. I am writing this chapter and thinking about how this writing itself is a working through, tracing the entanglements of grief and hope. I find myself holding my breath. I think about how I had told my sister that I wished, at every big life decision, that I could talk to Mom. Just to know what she would say. And even thinking this, my breath catches in my throat. I am holding my breath, I realize. Holding back the tears that still come, unasked for, involuntarily, in moments that catch me off-guard. Holding my breath because to think these things is to offer to work through them. Work through even as there is not necessarily an end in sight, there will not be a moment that I will reach where suddenly I will not feel grief. A moment when, to think about my impending graduation or a move to a new city, a new job, to think about the future, hazy with all its undefined possibilities, will not bring with it a mixture of joy and sadness. I am holding my breath, in the coffee shop as I realize that in this moment, this here-and-now, I cannot think motherhood without grief. Immobilized by her not-being-there-then. Even as I know that someday, this may not be the case, that if/when that moment happens, it will be another working through, and other feelings will become possible.

I am holding my breath. Writing about this other ending. An ending that feels so small in comparison to the big feelings of grief. I do not cry when I think about that ending, even as there are ways in which I am sad. I sat on my floor as I packed boxes and thought about the choice that I had made to end something in relation to an ending that I had no choice about. There are messy, complicated, contradictory feelings that go along with griefs big and small. And here I am, writing through them. Asserting my being-there, my becomings. Hoping.

* * *

FEBRUARY 20, 2012

Good things:

- Coconut rice.
- Going outside in the evening when you've been working all day and discovering it is beautiful outside.
- Starting new projects.
- Earl gray tea with milk and sugar.
- Weaving.
- Walking to work in February not wearing a coat.
- Freshly washed sheets.
- The feeling right after you wash your face before bed.

* * *

FEBRUARY 8, 2019

Things that are good:

- Flannel sheets.
- Being so immersed in something that you realize it has become dark and you have forgotten to turn the lights on.
- Driving with the windows down on an unexpectedly warm day.
- Seeing the lake emerge as you drive over the hill from Dundee to the point.
- The sound of rain at night when you have nowhere to be.
- Chocolate chips from the freezer.
- Cold cream when you open it for the first time.

- Being just cold enough to need a sweater, but not so cold that you're uncomfortable without it.
- Running in the morning when the sky is just starting to turn orange over the lake.
- The humid feeling of warmth in the car when you first get in it after it's been sitting in the sun (but only for the first few moments).
- Earl gray tea with milk and sugar.

REFERENCES

Ahmed, S. (2017). *Living a feminist life*. Durham, NC: Duke University Press.

Barad, K. (2017). Troubling time/s and ecologies of nothingness: Re-turning, re-membering, and facing the incalculable. *New Formations, 92*, 56–86.

Forby, M. (Director). (2009). *Princess Kaiulani* [Motion picture]. United States: Matador Pictures.

Lopez, R., & Marx, J. (2003). There's a fine, fine line [Stephanie D'Abruzzo]. In *Avenue Q 2003 Original Broadway Cast*. New York, NY: Masterworks Broadway.

Ozeki, R. L. (1999). *My year of meats*. New York, NY: Penguin Books.

Santos, M. de los. (2011). *Belong to me* (Reprint edition). New York, NY: Avon Books.

Shōnagon, S. (1991). *The pillow book of Sei Shōnagon* (I. Morris, Trans.). West Sussex, NY: Columbia University Press.

PART II

Navigating Grief and Narrating Hope
Through Writing

The Art of Bereavement: An Autoethnographic Reflection on Transformational Learning Following the Loss of a Spouse

Angela Kinder Mains

In 2013, my husband of nearly ten years, Jeremy—or Jer—was diagnosed with an aggressive form of lymphoma and given an undetermined prognosis. He spent significant time in the hospital receiving treatment and dealing with severe complications such as kidney failure, septic shock, a pulmonary embolism, and pneumonia. Additionally, the treatment plan for his lymphoma required intrathecal chemotherapy, a process that involved injecting high concentrations of chemotherapy directly into his brain. Over time, as a result of this particular treatment, Jer experienced seizures and full facial paralysis. Eventually he could not move his mouth to eat or smile, and he was unable to open or close his eyes. His face was emotionless, and it was difficult to gain any sense of what he was thinking or feeling at any given moment. His ability to speak intelligibly was strained, until eventually he was unable to talk at all. Three and a

A. K. Mains (✉)
West Chicago, IL, USA

© The Author(s) 2020
S. A. Shelton and N. Sieben (Eds.),
Narratives of Hope and Grief in Higher Education,
https://doi.org/10.1007/978-3-030-42556-2_6

71

half months after his diagnosis, as his body suffered the impact of chemo toxicity, Jer was placed on a ventilator, and we did not hear his voice again. His mind, however, was still quite active.

During those last weeks of his life, Jer became a prisoner in his own body, unable to talk or smile or cry, communicating only with hand motions such as thumbs up or down, and saying "I love you" by squeezing my hand three times—a trick that we had used many times throughout our marriage when speaking the words aloud had not been important. As he got weaker, I would use my own hands to manually pull his eyelids apart so he could see me as I spoke or show him daily videos of our children, hoping that this would give him just a little more strength to keep fighting, to stay strong. While his determination to fight and determination to, as he would say, stay "wide awake," never wavered, Jeremy died exactly five months after we first received his lymphoma diagnosis.

During Jer's illness, he endured weeks in the hospital and increased physical deterioration. I had to rapidly adjust to the new reality of not having him actively present in our lives. My new reality included supporting and encouraging Jer and visiting him as often as I could, while continuing to work full-time, and raise our three young children, ages 5 years old, 3 years old, and 7 months old, on my own. The stress, anxiety, and trauma of his illness had a tremendous impact on the choices that I made every day. I found myself constantly considering how to be fully present for my husband and children, while also looking ahead and anticipating a future without him. I was keenly aware that choices I was making in those moments could have a tremendous impact on how I, and more importantly, our children, would be able to grieve, heal, and grow during and after this tragedy.

I felt myself getting stronger each day as Jer got weaker. I felt braver, more centered, and focused. I was determined to *do this well*—i.e., I was determined to be the best version of myself that I could be during Jer's final months. This meant being fully present for Jer and enduring the painful days alongside him. It meant being fully present for my children, modeling what it looked like to live through very difficult days with strength and an awareness that not all would be lost. It meant being fully aware of myself and my needs, protecting us all from anything that would distract me from being what I needed to be in those final moments. I felt that I had to do my very best as a gift to Jer, demonstrating that all would be well on the other side of his illness. I needed to be my best, to find my strength, in order to lay a solid foundation for myself and our children once he was gone.

Looking back, I have often thought that I have never done anything so well in my life as living through the five months of Jer's illness and the months immediately after his passing. I am grateful and proud of that. However, since his death, I have frequently wondered why it was that I had to *find strength* and be my *best* for that particular time? Why had I not had strength or an ability to be *better* at other points in our marriage? What was it about myself, our marriage, or that situation that brought about the ability for me to engage in a new role within our relationship that had a significant and positive impact on my growth and identity but that came at such a high cost?

Autoethnography as Therapy

Three years after Jer died, I began to use autoethnography as a tool to make sense of this experience. According to Adams, Jones, and Ellis (2015), autoethnographic research begins with "epiphanies"—which are "transformative moments and realizations that significantly shape or alter the perceived course of our lives" (p. 49), which may be connected to traumatic experiences. Through careful, systemized analysis of the experience and one's thoughts and responses to it, the autoethnographer can create meaning or gain deeper understandings. This reflective, analytical process and the end product can be not only informative to existing research theory, but to healing as well. Autoethnography allows the researcher to embrace their own story while conducting research. As such, autoethnographic research has been called "a way of caring for the self" (Adams et al., 2015, p. 62).

In my case, I used personal writings and artifacts, including my personal journals and social media posts, to explore my experience with transformational learning and identity development following such a significant loss. My goal was to identify various epiphanies as a means to better understand not only my grief journey, but also the factors that contributed to my perceived personal growth during my husband's illness and following his death.

THEORETICAL PERSPECTIVE

My goal in using autoethnography as a tool to understand my experience was not simply to rewrite my experience but analyze it from a theoretical framework that aided me in documenting my process of self-discovery. I found that the feminist perspective was integral to my understanding of personal growth following my husband's death as I explored the roles we played within our relationship as husband and wife. The work of Simone de Beauvoir (1949) was particularly helpful as I analyzed my understanding of marriage and my relationship with Jer. de Beauvoir explained how young girls are raised to be women in response to "those that are men" and that "Man is the Subject; he is the Absolute. She is the Other" (p. 6). While analyzing my marriage using de Beauvoir's perspective, I discovered I had long maintained an unconscious acceptance of being the Other to Jer.

CONSTRUCTING OUR MARRIAGE

Prior to meeting Jer, I had grown up believing that when a man and woman were married, they became *one* and each represented the other. There was no individuality, no distinction in beings. Thus, I—unconsciously—believed that through marriage, my individuation would dissolve, and my identity would be directly connected to the nature of my husband's character and the state of our marriage. As I began to spend time with potential life partners, one thought often nagged me: Was that particular man worthy enough to absorb me? If over time we got married, could I become *one* with him? Was he the right person to give my agency to?

As I had come to understand marriage as a process of *being absorbed* by my spouse, I, naturally, wanted to find someone worthy enough to disappear into. When I met Jer, I immediately thought he was *better than me*, and I believed that through our union, I would become *better*, too. As I reviewed writings in my journals for my autoethnography, I noticed that this idea that Jer was better than me appears over and over again. Notes that I found from our pre-marital counseling sessions document that when asked, "Why do you want to marry this person?" I wrote, "I want to marry Jer because he is so much better than me." Thus, my adoration for Jer resulted in an unconscious abdication of my agency even before we were married.

These beliefs about the way in which I would relate to my husband through absorption are precisely what de Beauvoir (1949) described when she said that men marry seeking "an expansion" of themselves, while women integrate into his world (p. 442). More specifically, de Beauvoir described marriage as a process where a woman is "annexed to her husband's universe" as she "gives him her *person*" (de Beauvoir, 1949, p. 443). I had grown to believe it was *good* to be absorbed by my husband, and back then I would have even argued that finding my own identity before marriage, or maintaining any sense of individuation from Jer, was not a vital component of my long-term well-being.

A few months prior to marrying Jer, I began letting go of any personal hopes and expectations that I had had for my life that did not involve Jer or align with the life that we planned to share together. I made a list of all the things I would let go of in order to be with Jer. My list included things like: living close to my parents, having my dad coach my kid's little league team, and marrying someone who was intellectual but not able to fix broken appliances or make home repairs. I thought letting go of my hopes and expectations would mean that I could enter into our impending marriage free of conflict, open to wherever we decided to go together—as one. I engaged in the process completely on my own. I seriously doubt that Jer did anything similar. For some reason, I thought that I had to deny myself in order to make our marriage conflict-free. Thus, even before our marriage, I engaged in a process of abdication. While doing so, I began viewing harmony in our relationship as my responsibility, and my responsibility alone.

During the course of our marriage I continued to adore Jer while denying myself. While I loved my life with him, I began to strongly dislike myself and who I was becoming. In choosing to marry Jer, I had let go of so many of the things that I had wanted in life. The majority of the decisions we made together were based on Jer's ideas, hopes, and dreams. In my desire for harmony, I proactively sought to support him in his efforts to build the life he had always wanted for his family, while simultaneously sacrificing my own hopes and desires. Ten years into our marriage and three children later, I found that while I deeply loved him and the life we shared together, I was increasingly dissatisfied with *my* life, because I could not see *me* anywhere in it.

I began to share my frustrations with Jer but, at that time, did not have the insight to truly articulate what I was feeling. I told him that when I looked at my life, I recognized that I would never live in our house, work at my job, or raise children in certain ways, had I not married him. The more I considered those thoughts, the more confused I became. I truly believe I loved my life with Jer, but I just didn't like who I was apart from that life. I didn't understand how it was possible for such feelings to exist simultaneously. Jer was concerned and encouraged me to identify what I did want for *my* life. I did not know how to consider *my* life as separate from *our* life, or how to pursue changes in *my* life that I desired but would necessitate a change in *our* life together. Jer was concerned and patient, committed to supporting me as I wrestled with these feelings, but also confused as to what I was trying to express. By that point in our marriage, neither of us knew how to identify or change the unconscious behaviors that had brought us to that point in our relationship.

As we continued to consider what steps I could take to independently meet my own needs, neither of us were able to see that the life we shared together was the result of my ongoing commitment to deny myself in support of Jer's ideas or desires. I had consistently let things go that interfered with my ability to support Jer and the life he—and, at the time I would have said *we*—had desired for our family. For example, if I wanted to do something, like pursue graduate coursework, if that meant a major adjustment to our schedule or demand that Jer spend more time caring for our children, I was quick to let it go as soon as Jer protested. I had long been in the habit of assuming that I was responsible for maintaining harmony, so I was quick to ease Jer's discomfort and proactively agreed—at times even offered—to discontinue my pursuit of something that could potentially have a negative impact on him. I believed that if something I wanted was not a good idea for *all of us*, it was not good for me, either. Thus, I would deny myself, believing that I was doing it for the sake of *us*. In that way, I was living out de Beauvoir's (1949) description of marriage as a state of annexation for the woman, as I was absorbed into Jer's world while minimizing my own needs and desires apart from him.

During the last years of our marriage I would tell Jer how unhappy I was in myself even though I loved our life and my family more than anything else. I did not understand how I could love my life with Jer so deeply yet, when I considered my life on its own merits, how I did not like who I was as an individual. Neither Jer nor I could see that what I needed most was my agency and individuation restored and then integrated into our shared life. I did not know how to address my own needs without creating disharmony and challenging our relationship. This was the state of our marriage when we received Jer's lymphoma diagnosis.

LIVING AND DYING WITH LYMPHOMA

After Jer was diagnosed, he was admitted to the hospital and spent the majority of his remaining five months there. While enduring the stress and trauma of an uncertain future, two important things happened that greatly impacted our relational dynamic. First, as Jer was frequently incapacitated due to his medical treatments, I became the *voice* of our experience and was therefore able to craft the narrative of Jer's health and the state of our emotional well-being. For the first time in our marriage, I was not relying on Jer to take the lead and describe who we were. And, to my surprise, Jer loved how I represented us on social media and other forums, and he encouraged me to continue to write and share our story in my way. I loved being encouraged and wondered if it had always been so easy to please him or if his weakened state allowed for my agency.

The second significant aspect of Jer's illness was the ongoing transformation of our home life and the roles that we played as parents and partners. During the early days of his illness, we believed Jer would be home from the hospital frequently, but with a compromised immune system, and would need a safe place at home to rest and recuperate. I took the lead in organizing family and friends in an effort to rearrange our home to prepare for Jer's recovery. I made all of the decisions without consulting Jer. The more empowered I was, the more I enjoyed it, even though I was constantly scared and concerned for Jer and our future together.

Throughout Jer's illness I never felt burdened by caring for him, visiting him in the hospital, or taking on more responsibilities at home. In fact, I often tell people that it was during Jer's illness that I felt the most alive, the most engaged in each present moment, and the most aware of who I was and what I was meant to do. While I often felt overwhelmed and ill-equipped to do all that was required of me, I also felt more fully realized than I had felt in years.

As the expenses of Jer's illness increased, I began to prepare the house in case we needed to sell it. The exterior of our century-old home was a combination of beige siding and gray wood, with the paint peeling in several places. Deciding on changes to the exterior of our home was one of the most concrete examples of how my behavior changed during Jer's illness and increased incapacitation.

Jer was weak and recovering from pneumonia when I told him about painting the exterior of our house. We talked about painting it a neutral color like beige to match the siding, as that would be the most *sellable*.

A former version of myself would have readily agreed. But, four months into Jer's illness, something inside of me wanted to be bolder and less safe. I kept thinking about the color *Berry Wine*. It seemed an audacious choice; with Jer getting weaker in the hospital, audacious is what I wanted to be.

The dramatic aesthetic changes reflected the major shifts in our home life and family culture. I wrote online:

> One of the hardest but less obvious parts (of this journey) is knowing that the kids and I are doing OK and we are moving on with life. They are learning new things, growing up, and have adjusted to not having Jeremy around. Our sweet baby has lived 30% of her life since Jeremy's diagnosis and extended hospital stays. The culture in our home is slowly changing as a result of Jeremy's extended absence. It is a silent wound that I don't know is there until I look for it and then I feel its sharp sting. (Jeremy Angela Mains, 2013)

I grieved the loss of the family culture that we—or, rather, Jer—had created, while I celebrated the new culture that I was taking the lead to create. I felt empowered to make important decisions and changes, knowing that my choices would potentially impact my and my children's lives, without Jer's direct influence and presence. All of these changes became a part of the early stages of my transformation.

After His Death

My personal transformation continued on, perhaps with greater intensity, after Jer died, as I sought to intentionally embrace the pain of losing him. In a blog post I wrote one month after the funeral, titled *Beginning*, I described my intention of "going toward the pain" of Jer's death. I wanted to feel each wave of grief, "life pulling pus from an infection, letting it ooze out." I believed doing this would allow me to heal thoroughly, with fewer scars to address later. I described the pain as "much like the pain of a burn—it is wounding and making a deep, lasting impact while getting worse, much worse, before it gets better." The pain surprised me and came out of nowhere like a "body slam." Yet, I committed to feeling each moment of it and recognized that it would be *a continual and life-long process* (Mains, 2013).

I saw my grief as a new beginning and an opportunity to create new rituals. If I anticipated a more difficult day or situation on the horizon, such as Jer's birthday, or any other holiday, I would plan ahead as to what I would do to both grieve and celebrate. On Jer's birthday, December 12, my kids and I had a birthday party for him, complete with his favorite food, gingerbread. We watched home videos of Jer playing with the kids, our children beaming and fixated on the screen. Inside I felt hollow and wept in the rare moments when I found myself alone. It was difficult, but on that day, when I wasn't crying, my children and I laughed, sang, and danced.

My greatest temptation in those early days was a soft whisper that I heard daily in my head: If life after Jer's death was too hard, no one would fault me for checking out, abdicating some of the heavy responsibilities and letting others step in. I fought that temptation with a heightened awareness of each task at hand and a commitment to see them through. Planning new rituals was one part of this process.

I felt strong in my new role of single mother. I recognized that it was hard, yet I enjoyed the challenge—a tribute to my newfound strength. In another blog post I described how, in those early days, I had struggled to get three children out of bed and on the bus or to their sitter on time— all on my own. By 8:15 each morning, with each child where they were supposed to be, I would sit in my car alone and take a minute to praise myself, saying, "I am Superwoman!" while surprised, perhaps relieved, by my newly discovered strength.

I was fully aware that I was grieving and growing but recognized that I was not always able to do both at once. In a post from February 8, 2014, I described my fragmented state of being. I acknowledged the multiple emotions I would feel as if they fought for control of my being. I noted that, "I've been shattered into a million pieces that fall into a wide spectrum. I don't know what it feels like to be whole" (Mains, 2014). The more time away from Jer's death, the more I contemplated the various parts of *me* in relationship to and separated from him:

> There is a part of me that was dying for five months and eventually died on November 5. There is a part of me that is still dying. There is a part of me that is simply going through the daily motions of life, feeling nothing. But there is also a part of me that is enjoying these days for what they are. There is even a part of me that is actually happy, really happy, and excited about life, excited about the future. All of these are pieces of me

that have been discombobulated, pulled apart, leaving me shattered, fragmented. They don't function together; they are out of sync, leaving me at
their mercy. For me, grief is being broken and longing to be whole again
but not knowing how to put myself back together. (Mains, 2014)

Three months after Jer's death I found myself in a new phase of my journey. Initially, I had felt weary and devastated, yet strong. Then, I began
to doubt my newfound strength. I wondered if I could stay the course
of my journey to my new way of being. I realized how much harder it
was going to be. It was like the honeymoon stage of grief was over, and
I had entered into the more difficult part of the work. I recognized that
I did not actually know who, or what, I was supposed to be without Jer.
I wrote:

> My fragmented self doesn't know what it means to be me without Jeremy.
> I don't know exactly who I am and what I like or don't like anymore. Sim-
> ple, everyday choices are complicated. I would pick a certain ____ (color,
> food, movie, book, activity, etc.) because I know he'd like it too, not just
> because I liked it. And, I definitely wouldn't pick it if I know he would
> hate it. I feel like I have to get to know myself all over again, constantly
> asking and not readily knowing "What do I want to do? What movie do I
> want to watch?" That alone is hard and painful as I am learning that this
> new version of me has thoughts and feelings that weren't present before
> (why not?, I wonder) and it adds another layer of "work" to this process.
> (Mains, 2014)

As I continued to grieve, I began challenging some of the elements in
my dynamic with Jer and our family life. In my head, I began fighting
with my dead husband. I would find myself walking through the grocery store, filling my cart with items Jer would never buy, thinking: "I
know you think this is wasteful, but I'm gonna buy it anyway." I even
purchased cable in December, though I knew Jer was passionate about
raising our children without a TV. I relished the opportunity to confront
these specific things—things that Jer had wanted for our family culture
and to which I had acquiesced—but now without him present, I found
myself either laughing or crying as I argued with Jer in my head, knowing
full well I was guaranteed to *win*.

I continued to proactively make changes in our home and our family
systems. Within the course of six months, there was not a single room in
my house that I had not altered, even just a bit. I would walk through

each room, feeling proud, noting that I had finally made my house *my home*. I noted that it had once felt frumpy, like me, but was now restored and beautiful and had become my sanctuary. I did not make any of these changes as a means to erase Jer's touch. I did them to acknowledge, perhaps even celebrate, that I existed. While I had complained, not even a year prior, that I could not see myself anywhere in our house and family culture, once Jer died I saw the new version of myself, which I liked, everywhere.

Now, on the Other Side

It has now been five years since Jer died. My children and I are thriving. We still live in our home, in the town Jer loved. We talk about Jer often. Every couple of months one child will request that we watch home movies of Jer for a bit, and we do. We talk about him frequently, affirming how he would have liked a particular story we read, or we guess together what he would think of a new joke one of my children learned. Five years later, Jer is still present in our everyday lives.

Occasionally, my kids and I will talk about how much has changed. One child frequently points out how I rearranged all the furniture and that he remembers where things were when his dad was alive. The oldest child sometimes comments on how she does not remember really talking with me before Jer died. She reflects on this for a bit and then shares how glad she is that I am more involved in her life. I know exactly what she means: I am no longer passively participating in my home life; I actively create and engage with it, supporting my children in ways that I did not when Jer was alive.

I have often wondered how it is that Jer's illness and death could be both a traumatic and positive experience. On one hand, this appears to be such a confusing contradiction. But, looking back on how the transformation occurred, it makes perfect sense. While I do not know if I would have experienced transformation had Jer never gotten sick and died, I know that now, on the other side, I can see clearly how important it was that I proactively engaged my grief and embraced a new way of being during his illness, and following his death.

My autoethnographic writing was designed to help me make sense of the transformation I had experienced and to highlight the potential for grief to foster tremendous learning and personal growth. Embracing grief as a learning opportunity proved to be a precious resource that will shape my lifetime. To me, that is the essence of the art of bereavement.

REFERENCES

Adams, T. E., Holman Jones, S., & Ellis, C. (2015). *Autoethnography: Understanding qualitative research*. Oxford, UK: Oxford University Press.

de Beauvoir, S. (1949). *The second sex*. New York, NY: Vintage Books.

Jeremy Angela Mains. (2013, September 25). *Yesterday was one of the more difficult days* [Facebook update]. Retrieved from https://www.facebook.com/jeremyangela.mains/posts/10200717414843265.

Mains, A. (2013, December 5). *Beginning by ending well* [Web log post]. Retrieved from http://beautyinthemidstofcrisis.blogspot.com/.

Mains, A. (2014, February 8). *Fragmented* [Web log post]. Retrieved from http://beautyinthemidstofcrisis.blogspot.com/.

CHAPTER 7

All at Once: Writing Grief

James Burford

THE LAST DAY (MAY 23RD, 2018)

I recall the last day that my mother and I were both alive as a series of episodes. They are divided by a line: before and after.

Time has blurred the first episode of the last day. I don't remember ordinary things, like waking. All I know is that I was sitting in a freezing café on campus working at my laptop. I was at the café because I couldn't work in the chaos of my apartment, which was full of empty boxes and piles of things to sift through, and then to pack or discard. I had about one month left at the institution where I worked before I was due to move from Bangkok to a new position at a university in Melbourne. That day, I was working on a draft of a research report about the life and career experiences of foreign academics in Thai universities—just as I was about to stop using those words to describe myself.

The second episode of the last day was characterized by a gathering anxiety. While I was at the café I got a message, or maybe a call. My youngest brother Cam told me that Mum had been rushed to the hospital and was in the emergency department. This was alarming, but not

J. Burford (✉)
La Trobe University, Melbourne, VIC, Australia
e-mail: J.Burford@latrobe.edu.au

S. A. Shelton and N. Sieben (Eds.),
Narratives of Hope and Grief in Higher Education,
https://doi.org/10.1007/978-3-030-42556-2_7

terrifyingly so. Mum had been sick for many years and had returned from the emergency department so many times that it felt ordinary to me. I had begun to think of her as tough and wiry—not invincible, but almost. I kept my laptop screen up to receive messages from my brother and used my phone to call my friend Nina in Christchurch. We spoke for a long time about illness, and distance and what to do, and when I was feeling better, I decided to walk back to my apartment.

It was hot on campus, but still I walked quickly under the cover way. As I was walking, an awful thought occurred to me. Since I was moving countries, I had decided not to keep some of the sacred objects that friends had given me over the years. Mostly these were small dolls or trinkets, to provide luck and ward off accidents. My friend Lock had gone to Japan and arrived back with two Daruma dolls for me—hollow, round, red, papier-mâché dolls. The eyes of Daruma dolls are usually blank when they are sold. As the recipient of the doll, I was told that it was my job to fill in one eye upon making a wish, and then I was to fill in the other eye upon its fulfillment. As I recalled, I had drawn a big black dot in the eye of one of the dolls with the hope of getting a new job. I filled in the second doll's eye with a prayer about the health of my family. Since I was about to leave Bangkok and nothing else untoward had happened, I thought the wishes must have come true and filled in the eyes of both dolls. Some days before, I had left the dolls on campus near a large tree where people tend to place sacred objects that can't be thrown away. My awful thought repeated: "I have tempted fate by filling in the eye too soon. It's my fault. I am killing my mother." I crossed a bridge to a *san phra phum* (*spirit house*, in Thai) on campus, a popular place for students to come around exam time. I was alone, and I knelt to pray. I prayed to the spirits to protect my mother: "I am sorry, please keep her safe."

The third episode of the last day was such an intense wave that I can only write it in the present tense. It is made up of Facebook messages and phone calls to my family and friends. At some point, I ask Dad if I should book a ticket home, and he says he thinks it would be a good idea; it doesn't look good. I find a ticket, but my credit card won't go through. I get my boyfriend to book the ticket, with a return date in two weeks just in case. I am rushing. I book with my regular airline, without checking others. It's still eight hours until my flight. My family is gathering at the hospital. My boyfriend arrives and helps me pack my bag; I am cold, and I am crying. My mother is struggling to breathe. I take a taxi to Suvarnabhumi Airport.

In the fourth episode, Mum dies. My brother Miles calls while I am at the airport in Bangkok, and for at least half a minute I pretend that I can't see him calling. Somehow I know, but I need to pretend she is still alive. I quietly collect my tray of food and deliver it to my table where my boyfriend is waiting for me. I call Miles back. She is dead. I don't know what else we say. My nose runs; my eyes run. I can't remember doing it, but I make it through security and board a plane. I am lucky to be seated alone at the end of an empty flight. I weep into a cushion. No one seems to notice, or they pretend that they don't. I transfer in Sydney. I arrive in Christchurch.

At some point during the flight, this day changes to the next. It is no longer the last day that my mother and I are both alive.

THE DAY AFTER (MAY 24TH, 2018)

Yesterday Mum died
I was in the queue at Burger King
When my brother called to give me the word
The airport was loud and busy
My boyfriend hugged me
And we cried at the money exchange
Mistaken for separating lovers
Which we are
He has no visa
So it's a trip I'm making alone

Today, I'm in Christchurch
Flying overnight, I
Arrived to my family cleaning
Taking before and afters of the cupboard doors
I lit the fire
And now my mother's eulogy is ringing in my ears
I find myself
Turning off the lights and compulsively pacing around
Bumping into objects strewn here and there
Navigating somehow

I knock the side table
A torch falls off
And turns on
I follow the path of light to the couch

And lie down
Try to sleep before
Morning arrives

The Next Two Weeks

I spend time with my family. I look through pictures. I find old letters. I talk to my friends. We get Mum's ratty dog groomed. My friends drive me places. Sometimes I sob gently, and sometimes they need to stop the car. I vacuum and re-vacuum the floor. We plan the funeral. I don't want to be a pallbearer. I talk to Mum in her coffin. I give a speech. People say it's a good speech. I have important conversations with my brothers. I sort through her things. I want to feel less hungry. I try on her rings. I find a letter Mum had written for me when I was a baby. I ask my friend to cancel her ticket to visit me. I walk outside with bare feet and listen to the cows. I worry about moving countries. I wonder if I am doing grief properly. I want to say that I remember hearing irrigators ticking, but it was winter, so that seems unlikely.

June 10th, 2018

I email accommodation services at La Trobe University to book a temporary room in Melbourne for the month of July. I see a story about the history of the campus. It was built on the site of an old hospital for the "insane," and the campus is littered with buildings associated with this past. There are rumors that people's bones lie beneath, but the scientists can't find the evidence. I keep searching online. There is a story about the ghost of a dead girl who haunts a building by constantly playing with a music box that was confiscated from her. Still, I'm searching. The traditional owners of the land are the Wurundjeri people. Before colonization, a bushland flourished.

June 20th, 2018

I'm back in Bangkok. Grief windows open unexpectedly: after a dream; when I'm too tired; when I finish part of a report and have a rush of relief. I'm packing boxes and finding it hard to throw anything away—will *this* trigger a memory? Will *that*? Sometimes our people live in our things. The window opens onto a kind of thinking I'm not used to: "If mum arrives in a dream, does she live in my pillow? Should I take it just in case?" I ask my friends and my boyfriend. I pack the pillow.

Revisions (Date Unknown)

I'm working on revisions for a paper that I have drafted with an Australian friend. We are writing about how caring for others shaped the spaces where we wrote our PhDs in. My friend is a single parent, and she wrote her PhD in her walk-in wardrobe. I did my PhD research in many places, but for about one year I wrote it on my Mum and Dad's old bed, while I was Mum's full-time caregiver. I notice that I am sitting in the same café on the day that I found out Mum was in the emergency room. I weep quietly as I make the revisions. I add a line dedicating the piece to my Mum.

Moving (July 1st, 2018)

I make it to Australia. I had visited here for holidays and for conferences, but I never saw myself living here. Somehow I could never imagine its dirt getting under my fingernails. My darling came with me. It was his first international trip. We took a photo at the airport to send his Mum. My Mum is dead. I try not to think about it.

When we arrive it is cold. As usual, I have over-prepared us and we sweat in gloves and scarves. We get lost trying to find a taxi. We get lost trying to find our room. We are dropped off on a Sunday. We can't find the reception office, so I leave my boyfriend with our bags and set off to find it. I take off in one direction and find my way into a housing development. Finally, one freezing hour later I speak to a student who directs me down the hill to campus.

When I arrive, the campus is full of hundreds of shrieking birds. It is beautiful. I skip a little bit as I make my way to pick up the key.

Email (The First Week of July)

I start work. In the first week, I get an email from a family member, and I start to cry. I am sobbing in my office, and I close the door. I have to get outside before anyone sees me. Someone smiles kindly as I rush toward the exit.

I have to organize an orientation day for new graduate researchers, even though I am profoundly disoriented. Every time that I email a new person, I let myself go for a walk to the ponds on campus. I wonder if people are curious as to why I have so many errands to run.

FLOODED

Flooded
I'm flooded
From the inside up
Neck deep
And thinking how did I get here?
I'm sodden
Leave a damp trace
Everywhere I go
Squishy and vulnerable

I MEET A COLLEAGUE

I meet a colleague who lost a parent around the same time as me. Sitting under an umbrella on campus, I feel like we are coming out to each other as people in mourning. She has just started her new job, too. As time nears for us to return to the office, we change the topic to something lighter. We are companions, and we move on.

THE NEXT FEW MONTHS

Moving on. My boyfriend did extend his stay, but at some point he needed to go back to Bangkok to take up a doctoral scholarship. I realize that he had been the one holding things together since we arrived. Once he leaves, I discover that I never figured out the buses, and I can't remember how to cook. I make sense of the route to get to work, and then these are the three places that I let myself go: home, bus stop, work. Sometime later I add the supermarket. For months I wonder why I don't cook for myself, until I realize that I never bought any pans. I order them online so that I don't have to go anywhere. I bury myself in work, arriving early and staying late. I come to campus every weekend. There are so many things, yes. But mostly it is that this is a place I know. Eventually, I dare myself to go new places. I start on campus. I gradually expand the list of places where I will let myself go.

I think about myself and how I am doing. The fact that this campus used to be an asylum is not lost on me. I talk to my friends on the phone often and mostly tell them the truth. My first assessment is that things aren't quite right. But also I think this is to be expected. I scan my body: mostly numb and sometimes noticing. And then I remember that my feelings are also quite close to the skin, and tears often leak out. I know that at some point things will settle down but I don't know when that will be. I imagine I will feel better in summer. I hear myself say things like, "My grieving process has been interrupted by moving countries, cities and jobs," and "I want to work through my grief." The truth is that I am worried about what will happen to me later if I don't look grief in the eye. I am scared of the power of my grief.

Linen

I notice that somehow my bedroom is connected to grieving. I buy all new white linens. In fact, everything I buy for my new room is white.

Partner

My partner is a doctoral student in Thailand. I have moved from Thailand to Australia in order to work as a lecturer who helps graduate students learn about research. Even though I know that we both agreed to this arrangement, in lower moments I feel like I have abandoned him when it is my turn to see him through his PhD; he saw me through mine. If love has languages, then ours are touch and time. So, we weren't sure how we were going to navigate a long-distance relationship. But so far it's been fine. I call my partner multiple times each day, often during lunchtime, when I take the bus, and when I walk home from work. We almost never argue. There was only one time that we did. I tried to describe my limited movements here and my concerns about them. "Why don't you just go somewhere else?" he asked. "If it was that simple I would," I reply. He can't understand why I am stuck, and I can't understand why I can't explain this to him. "His Mum is still alive," is what I think to myself.

Face Cream

I don't want to use the last of my face cream. I bought it when I came back to New Zealand to graduate. Mum was alive then, and now she's not. I use tiny amounts carefully, measuring it out on the back of my hand. I wonder how I will feel when all the face cream is gone. I think of my mother applying face cream to my grandmother's face as she was dying. I think about how I never saw Mum's body, how everyone advised me not to. I wonder who I am saving the face cream for.

Working with Grief

I see a call for chapters for a book on writing narratives about hope and grief in the academy. I think that this will be a good project. I already research the affective world of the university, but I have never written about grief. I decide to take my grief on as a project that I will try to be curious about. I decide that I want to work with my grief in a way that isn't just living inside it.

October 29th, 2018

I speak at a conference for higher degree researchers about academic futures. I speak about the unpredictability of academic lives, and how I am still adjusting to my most recent international movement. I don't talk about grief exactly, but I feel like it is always leaking out of me. I am given a gift voucher to thank me for speaking. I go home and do a web search for books about grief. I use the voucher to buy five books. I don't want to borrow books from the library. I want the grief books to be mine. Buying the books is some kind of commitment.

Reading Grief

The place I am living has a bathtub, and since I am reluctant to explore new places, I spend a lot of time in it. I buy essential oils, scented candles, bath salts, bath oils, body scrubs. The bath is where I go to read about grief. If I am honest, I have to say that I find it easy to *start* reading books on grief and harder to *finish* them.

I re-read Laurel Richardson's (2007) *Last Writes: A Daybook for a Dying Friend*. I choose this book because it is a story about loss and also a story about writing. Laurel Richardson is a sociologist, and she uses her Daybook to investigate concerns like friendship, loss, aging, and the lived experiences of academic women. It is also a vehicle to process stress and fear and anxiety about the death of her best friend, and fellow academic, Betty. As she says,

> Writing in the Daybook helped me get through the final nine months of Betty's life. Writing kept me alive to the immanence of illness in her life—and its shadow on mine. Keeping the Daybook was therapeutic. It gave me a space to vent my emotions, record her end of life stories, our shared experiences, and chronicle the "good days and bad days" phenomenon of chronic illness—and wellness. (Richardson, 2007, p. 170)

I wonder if this is what I am doing in undertaking this project? Is this a space to vent? I don't feel that this is quite the right word to describe my warm-up. I really enjoy Richardson's book. Her writing is direct, her cast of characters are real living people, and her observations are unflinching. But I know this won't be how I write this chapter; I will flinch, and I'll try not to write too much about other people. Curiously, Richardson's (2007) book is also a story of arriving in Melbourne for a short-term academic visit. Some of her observations about my new city connect with me, but many of them don't. I find myself struggling to recognize the Melbourne that she evokes in her story. I think about the different bodies that we inhabit, my own upbringing Down Under, how all of this orients me to the world. After I finish her book, I feel like I have done something.

Not Reading Grief

I carry around Joan Didion's (2005) book *The Year of Magical Thinking* in my bag. I read it twice while Mum was sick. I love this book, but now it is just another weight in my bag. I struggle to know when I am letting myself off the hook and when I should keep myself on there wriggling. This time I slide myself off.

These are all the other books that I bought and didn't finish reading:

- *A Grief Observed* by C. S. Lewis.
- *Nora Webster* by Colm Tóibín.
- *A Widow's Story* by Joyce Carol Oates.
- *Levels of Life* by Julian Barnes.
- *Say Her Name* by Francisco Goldman.

Writing Grief

This chapter has tracked my ordinary experiences of living with the grief of my mother's death: leaving a job I loved, shifting between countries, adjusting to a new academic position in a new place, and missing my partner who stayed put as I moved. The first part of the title, *All at Once*, gestures to the compressed timeframe of many of these events. The second part of the title, *Writing Grief*, identifies writing as a practice that I have embraced in order to stay afloat, explore my experience, and attend to the lessons that grief and change may have to teach me. The words above trace how grief shaped, and was absorbed into, my changing academic life. Attentive readers might have noticed some shiftiness in terms of the verb tenses across this piece. When we write grief, what episodes are past and what is present, continuous? I don't know the answer, but my grief has required a wobbly kind of grammar.

In this closing section, I want to argue that the *process* of writing these words was valuable in-and-of itself *as a process*. By approaching my grief with the practice of writing, I have spun myself to a web of scholars who view writing as a mode of inquiry (Richardson & St. Pierre, 2005) to assist them to find out more about themselves. As Richardson (1994) suggests, writing is not only a "mopping-up activity" that researchers might do at the end of a formal project; it is also a "way of 'knowing'—a method of discovery and analysis" (p. 516). These ideas about writing as a personal process of discovery also connect to popular books, such as *The Artist's Way* (Cameron, 1992), *Writing Down the Bones* (Goldberg, 1986), and *Bird by Bird* (Lamott, 1995). Each of these authors has advocated for writing to be understood as a way of finding out about oneself, as well as an everyday creative and spiritual practice that we can engage in when times are tough. They also have fantastic prompts or suggestions for those who are trying to find ways in or encouragement. While I was aware of all of these available resources for thinking about writing, some of the key sources of inspiration for this project came from academics who have written about their own lives. Here I am thinking of projects like Les Back's (2016) *Academic Diary*, which presents a collection of diary entries reflecting on the changes and continuities of academic life. Back weaves together a critical analysis of what is changing in universities—for good and ill—and reminds us of why higher education still matters.

A second source of inspiration for writing this chapter came in the form of Ann Cvetkovich's (2012) book *Depression: A Public Feeling*. Like

Back, Cvetkovich reflected on her own academic life and sought to record what living in depression felt like, as well as how she moved through this feeling by altering the routines and rhythms of her daily life. Like Cvetkovich, much of my healing is at that ordinary level—from the linen on my bed, to the salts in my bath. My story is one of making my life small, predictable, and full of sensory pleasures, in order to cope with significant upheavals in my life.

In offering these *private* feelings a public airing, it has been my goal to offer company to others who find themselves in similar places. Additionally, I hope that by sharing some of the ordinary practices that I have used, colleagues might discern ways of being in grief that they can try themselves. To all who have read this chapter, I want to say, "I wish you well."

February 10th, 2019

A thought comes to me: I should try and be alive now, go for a walk in the sunshine or something. And that is what I do.

For my mother, Vicki Anne Dalzell.

References

Back, L. (2016). *Academic diary: Or why higher education still matters*. London, UK: Goldsmiths Press.

Cameron, J. (1992). *The artist's way: A spiritual path to higher creativity*. New York, NY: Putnam.

Cvetkovich, A. (2012). *Depression: A public feeling*. Durham, NC: Duke University Press.

Didion, J. (2005). *The year of magical thinking*. New York, NY: Alfred A. Knopf.

Goldberg, N. (1986). *Writing down the bones: Freeing the writer within*. Boston, MA: Shambhala Press.

Lamott, A. (1995). *Bird by bird: Some instructions on writing and life*. New York, NY: Anchor Books.

Richardson, L. (1994). Writing: A method of inquiry. In N. Denzin & Y. Lincoln (Eds.), *Handbook of qualitative research* (pp. 516–529). Thousand Oaks, CA: Sage.

Richardson, L. (2007). *Last writes: Daybook for a dying friend*. Walnut Creek, CA: Left Coast Press.

Richardson, L., & St. Pierre, E. A. (2005). Writing: A method of inquiry. In N. K. Denzin & Y. S. Lincoln (Eds.), *The Sage handbook of qualitative research* (pp. 959–978). Thousand Oaks, CA: Sage.

CHAPTER 8

The Refrains That Help Me Remember: An Autoethnography of Grief, Epistemological Crisis, and Discovering Hope Through Theory

Boden Robertson

On May 24, 2018, an impaired driver drifted onto the shoulder of a road in Glencoe, Alabama, striking two Auburn University students who had been participating in a geology field dig (Feringa, 2019). One victim was my best friend, Nick. His sister, who was just setting out on a four-hour frantic drive toward University of Alabama-Birmingham Hospital in Birmingham, Alabama, where emergency personnel had airlifted him, called me. Details were scant. Presuming no one would be there for his sister when she arrived, I left immediately. It was a rare weekend, because I happened to be in Tuscaloosa, an hour away. I had spent most weekends that semester in the hospital with my dad in Dothan, about 185 miles away. Earlier that year in January, I had received a similar frantic call while my brother had driven our father to the hospital, which began

B. Robertson (✉)
The University of Alabama, Tuscaloosa, AL, USA
e-mail: wbrobertson@crimson.ua.edu

© The Author(s) 2020
S. A. Shelton and N. Sieben (Eds.),
Narratives of Hope and Grief in Higher Education,
https://doi.org/10.1007/978-3-030-42556-2_8

95

Dad's nine-month battle with necrotizing fasciitis (NF). During this time, I felt like I was being pulled in multiple directions: doctoral coursework in Tuscaloosa, visiting Nick in Birmingham, and visiting Dad in Dothan. As a result of the injuries Nick sustained, he went into a coma and clung to life for 39 days. Nick passed away on June 30 at 31-years-old. Three months later, on September 25, Dad passed away at 69-years-old. Having lost my grandparents and mother in recent years, I found the size of my support system and family shrunken. I felt isolated and alone.

Due to the incredible compassion of my advisor and professors, I was able to continue my coursework at my own pace. Without this, I would not have been able to continue. One asked me to write this chapter, but while I had certainly experienced the grief, I struggled to find hope. I found it through autoethnography.

I start this chapter by detailing my struggle to accurately remember the lives of the two people dearest to my heart. I then discuss finding the deleuzoguattarian concept of the refrain and how it served as a tool to claim my memory. The chapter then closes with three vignettes constructed through the autoethnographic process of refrain. I wanted to give both people's memories the space that they deserved, but in this chapter I share the refrains of my father.

A METHODOLOGICAL STRUGGLE OF REMEMBERING

I wanted to tell a story. Being familiar with the work of Carolyn Ellis and Art Bochner through coursework, autoethnography was the logical choice. Autoethnography is "an autobiographical genre of writing and research that displays multiple layers of consciousness, connecting the personal to the cultural" and has increasingly become accepted as a central form of social science research (Ellis & Bochner, 2000, p. 739). Knowing this, I dug through my notebooks, reviewed what I had learned, and began to reflect on the worst year of my life.

Autoethnography uses three central forms of data collection: fieldnotes, personal documents, and interviews. As the events had already happened, personal documents included social media posts and texts about my father's and Nick's hospitalizations. Those documents triggered memories from which I composed fieldnotes as event recollections. Anderson and Glass-Coffin (2013) write that this form of recollection provides "opportunities for reflexive engagement in the fieldnotes themselves" (p. 67). This reflexivity was key to my remembering, as I engaged in informal interviews—that were more conversations—with my brother. During the process, I re-recalled and re-remembered the grief, struggle, and memories of the last year.

I started by chronologically recording my memories. Afterward, I found that I had written two exceptionally long obituaries. They were boring and lacked any trace of humanity. Attending a workshop on autoethnography hosted by Ellis and Bochner changed this.

One jotting I made during the seminar read: "Don't make it linear, make the story talk back, write it down, question it, criticize it, leave it, come back to it, question it again, criticize it again." Then in all caps: "DO THE OTHERS IN OUR LIVES JUSTICE." Doing this was a struggle. The methodological openness of autoethnography can be simultaneously liberating and challenging. Relying on my jottings from the workshop, I set about rereading my notes and attempting to form a cohesive narrative to tie them together. A crisis occurred when I thought about my alignment with postmodern theory and how it impacts conceptualizations of memory.

At its core belief, postmodernism embraces plurality and doubts singularity. When applied to discourse, Richardson (1994) wrote that postmodernism works against a "universal and general claim as the 'right' or the privileged form of authoritative knowledge. Postmodernism suspects all truth claims of masking and serving particular interests" (p. 517). I had my memories, but my postmodern epistemology challenged their authenticity and accuracy. Ethically, I wondered if I was doing their lives justice by focusing only on my own self-interest. I started to think of my memories as unstable, incomplete, and partial-at-best (Lincoln, 1997), and I brought these concerns up in a conversation with my brother:

> I talked with my brother today about how writing this project interferes with my memory. Countless stories from his friends and others around the time of his death are clouding my memory. My memories are becoming infused with others'. Stories of his strength and skill in sports and coaching are mingling with the compassion he showed me when I came out to him, and I hate it. Its chaos. I resent the memories of others. I want to remember him for me, but ethically I'm not sure about it. I think I read too much, and I'm too far into my own head. How much should I allow theory to creep into real life? (Fieldnote, June 15, 2019)

Was I being selfish by insisting on the prominence of my own memory? Surely, others' memories of my father and Nick were just as valid. I came across a writing by Abrams (2010) that made me pause: "Memory is not just about the individual; it is also about the community, the collective, and the nation" (pp. 78–79). I wanted to consider others but felt this detracted from my own memories. I wanted to be selfish. Frustrated, I walked away from the project and contemplated quitting it altogether.

THANK YOU, PAUL KLEE

A *Thousand Plateaus* (*ATP*) has been sitting on my bookshelf since my Ph.D. study introduced me to postmodernism. I would sometimes pick it up, read a little, find myself feeling woefully ill-equipped to understand it, detest it as too complex, abstract, and aloof, and I would put it away. But like a glutton for punishment—i.e., graduate student—I have kept reading.

I had decided to give up on writing this chapter but toiled over the decision for a week. During this time, I picked up *ATP* and thumbed through it. Having encountered Paul Klee's work through studying German, Plateau 11's title page with Klee's *Twittering Machine* caught my eye. The authors wrote, "The role of the refrain has often been emphasized: it is territorial, a territorial assemblage. Bird songs: the bird sings to mark its territory. The Greek modes and Hindu rhythms are themselves territorial, provincial, regional" (Deleuze & Guattari, 1987, p. 312). Refrains territorialize the world and help us make sense of where we are. These repetitive and rhythmic patterns are all around us. Refrains help slow the chaos around us. The author's example of a boy lost in the dark, humming to himself, perfectly exemplifies the attempt to bring comfort to oneself by slowing the chaos. I thought about the chaos of remembering. I set out to find the refrains that could slow the chaos, help me remember, and tell a story worth telling.

These vignettes are the refrains of my father. For me, refrains came in the form of sayings that my father consistently used as words of wisdom. These refrains helped me to make sense of my memories, to claim the territory they demarcate, and to remember his impact on me. This is how I remember.

A Refrain to Remember, Part 1

You've only got one person in the world to please, and that's yourself—Dad, countless times

I realized that I was different around the age of 12 when my desires did not conform to other boys' lewd whispers at school. Like countless others growing up differently in the Deep South, I hid my true self from loved ones and friends. I became adept at going with the flow and reading people's intentions. I became an expert in deception. The open hostility of the social world I inhabited ingrained the importance of "passing" from an early age. The consequence of fitting-in was feeling beholden to others' expectations, particularly my father's.

I thought he wanted me to be like him, to play sports. I thought that he wanted me to be tough and strong like him. Throughout my life, Dad's friends and colleagues regaled me with stories of his extraordinary strength in the weight room, explosiveness on the football field, and exceptionality in coaching football defense. These stories conditioned me to view my father one-dimensionally: the rough and rugged football coach; the epitome of the hypermasculine Southern man; feared by no one; respected by all. I deeply feared not living up to his expectations.

Dad was well-known in our small town. His giant-like stature and deep voice commanded attention. With an intimidating yell of "Hey!" he melted the spines of senior boys standing face-to-face preparing to fight. The crowd around them cheering for blood would immediately disperse. Fights did not happen when Dad was on break duty. He was an educator and football coach who loved his students as if they were his own. After his passing, a high school friend messaged me on Facebook:

> Coach was the epitome of a gentle giant. He was very instrumental to me as a young kid and was a mentor to a lot of us boys and girls who walked the halls. Thank you for sharing your dad with us! His impact will be felt for years to come! (Facebook Message, September 25, 2018)

I played football in junior high because I thought it was what he wanted. Truthfully, I hated every single moment of it. The 9th grade had ended, summer was upon us, and the grueling two-a-day practices were soon beginning for varsity football. I decided to tell Dad that I would not keep playing. I feared the worst: his disappointment.

That day, standing on our back porch, I was numb. I couldn't feel the sweltering heat around me nor the thick balminess that makes walking during Alabama summers resemble wading through soup. My voice had cracked under the pressure, but I managed to get the words out of my trembling fourteen-year-old mouth.

"Why?" he asked.

I gulped and felt the stickiness of fear in the back of my throat. "I don't like it. I don't understand it. I don't want to play anymore." I awaited the worst.

"I've seen you play, and I can tell your heart isn't in it," he said.

"He thinks I suck," I thought.

My voice trembled. "I'm sorry, Dad. I'm so sorry."

The emotions I had held back until then bubbled to the surface, and I started crying. He put his huge arms around me, and I sobbed.

"Listen. Calm down, buddy. It's okay," he said comfortingly. "I love you. You shouldn't be this upset about it."

Wiping the tears from my face, I told him my greatest fear. "I just don't want to disappoint you, Dad."

He said something to me that I had heard him say often but would come to hold great meaning to me later in life: "Bo, you've only got one person in this world to please, and that's yourself."

A Refrain to Remember, Part 2

You're my favorite dog, even if you never win a race.—Dad, countless times

I had no plan after high school, except knowing I should attend college. I followed a friend's interest and moved with him to attend the University of Alabama. Tuscaloosa, while certainly no bastion of progressivism, was liberating compared to my hometown. I started the process of coming out and finding myself. It was the first time that I got to be me. In Tuscaloosa, I was no longer my father's son. I was just me, and I loved being me. I met friends who did not care about my sexuality. I formed a stand-in family in Tuscaloosa. It was easy to come out to those I had recently met, but I lacked the strength to come out to those I had lied to. My greatest fear in coming out to Dad was that he would be embarrassed of me. Others would surely snicker about him behind closed doors for having a gay son. Over the years, this fear had caused me to drift from my father and my family. I checked in infrequently by phone and visited home only on holidays.

As time went on, I felt an immense guilt for being distant. I knew that I lacked the courage to tell Dad in person. I decided that if I was going to do it, it must be over the phone. One spring night, at 27-years-old, I stepped out on my balcony and called him.

He answered the phone in his typical gruff and overexaggerated, "Hey there, boy!" that since his passing, my brother and I invoke in our phone conversations to remember him. We talked about the weather, Crimson Tide Football, and what was going on in my hometown. The conversation was normal, but Dad knew something was going on.

"You alright?" he asked.

"Yeah, I'm okay. But there's something I want to talk to you about."

After a brief pause, he said, "All right. Well hell, tell me."

I laughed nervously, took a deep breath, summoned up my courage and said it.

I nervously awaited his response. My mind raced into a thousand negative responses: being disowned, losing my family, etc.

He chuckled, "Bo, I don't mean to take the wind out of your sails or anything, but it's kinda something I've known for a while."

"Really?"

"Well, you can't go this long without dating a girl and having as many girl friends as you do and 'ol dad not wonder about it."

I laughed nervously and started to cry, peace and calm washing over me. "I was so scared to tell you because I don't want you to be embarrassed of me," I said.

He assuaged my fears by saying something he had often said to me: "Bo, you're my favorite dog, even if you never win a race."

That night on the phone, I learned more about Dad than I had ever known. He shared a story about accepting his first coaching job in 1972 at a high school in Atlanta. Through working a side job delivering flowers to florists, he met gay men for the first time. He told me that until then, his only concept of gay men had come from stories about bearded men lurking in bus station bathrooms. Through these friends, he realized that what others had told him was wrong.

He shared stories about police raids on gay bars to shame patrons and drag performers, and the damaging effects they had had on his friends. His friends shared stories of hardship after their families abandoned them.

He sympathized with them. He sympathized with me, telling me that he knew it must have been hard on me growing up.

"I really wished I could've known and been there for you," he said.

"It was bad, but I made it through by pretending to not be different," I said.

He paused for a few seconds.

"Bo," he said in a strained voice, "if I ever made a joke or a comment that made you feel that I wasn't in your corner, I'm so sorry for that. I love you so much."

His voice was rich with kindheartedness. I don't think that my dad had ever apologized to me.

A terrible emotion of regret and loss struck me. My voice started cracking as I put my thoughts into words. "I regret not believing you could love me being gay. I've always known that you love me. I was just so scared." The emotions got the best of me, and I sobbed.

He told me how proud he was that I finally told him the truth, which in turn made me cry even more. We made an agreement that night to never keep anything from each other, to rely on each other, and to get to know each other again. We both acknowledged that it would take time, but that it was something we both deeply wanted.

Over the years, we rebuilt our relationship. I never dreamed that one day I would take a significant other home to meet my dad, but the old football coach of gigantic stature was warm and welcoming to him. When we broke up, I depended on Dad for advice and comfort. When I was single, he would ask me how the dating was. My sexuality was far from the main topic of our conversations, but it was something that he was not embarrassed by and did not avoid.

A Refrain to Remember, Part 3

Your greatest failures in life are those where you give up on yourself. Don't you ever sell yourself short.—Dad, countless times

Reconnecting with Dad had been great, and we had many conversations about my future. I decided that I wanted to be a teacher and enrolled in a German M.A. program at the University of Alabama. During my first semester, my mother was diagnosed with Stage IV stomach cancer. Doctors gave her one month to live and did not recommend treatment. I left Tuscaloosa and my classes to be with her. She refused to not seek treatment, going against doctors' orders, determined to live. She fought for seven months, losing half of her body weight and all of her beautiful red hair to chemo. She passed away on July 2, 2015, one month before I was set to go to Germany for a year to shore up my language skills.

I set out for Germany emotionally wounded but strived to focus on my studies and enjoy life again. Soon after arriving, I learned my partner back-home had been cheating on me. This, coupled with the loss of my mother, was decimating. I leaned heavily on Dad during this time, calling him often and seeking advice. I returned to the United States after my year abroad with plans to later pursue a Ph.D. in German or second language acquisition. The hardship of loss took a toll on my well-being. The GRE prep books on my bookshelf next to my desk taunted me. I was floundering. I could not focus. My teaching was lackluster. My performance in classes was dismal. I earned my first B in a class. I was drowning. I registered for the GRE and took the test without studying. It had been a decade since I had taken a math class. My score was seven points below the admissions requirement. The graduate school rejected my application. It crushed the little self-esteem I was desperately clinging to.

I wanted to run away. I had failed my professors' expectations. I was embarrassed to see people in my cohort. I ducked through hallways to avoid making eye contact with my advisor. Distraught, I called dad. I was frantic. I was crying. The dream of pursuing a career in higher education was crumbling around me.

"I've failed, Dad. I can't even pass the GRE. I'm so ashamed. Comps are in a month. I've got no time for GRE prep. Applications for assistantships need to be in ASAP. This isn't going to work." I was beside myself.

"Calm down, Bo," he said. He waited for me to stop. "It's going to be okay, man."

"I need advice, Dad," I said steadying my emotions.

"First, you got nothing to be ashamed of. Those tests don't measure you. They're a hurdle. It's a tick of a box that shows that you aren't just some jack-leg student."

I laughed. It always made me laugh when he referred to someone as a "jack-leg" anything.

"I know, but I don't think I can do it. There's no way. There's no time."

"Is this something you want? To get your PhD?" he asked.

"Yes," I replied.

"Well listen, I'm gonna tell you like I used to tell my boys in the fourth quarter. Look, your back is against the wall. You want it and so does that hostile individual that's lined up in front of you."

I laughed. I always laughed when he referred to an opposing player as a "hostile individual."

He laughed and continued, "It comes down to who wants it more, you or him. But, whatever the outcome, when that hostile individual is walking off the field, the one thing he's gonna know for damn sure is that you didn't take it lying down. So, if this is what you want, you've gotta fight for it. You've gotta show them that you want it. You gotta fight his ass for every inch."

I studied for comprehensive exams, and I studied for the GRE. It was grueling. But, I passed my written comps. One week later, I took the GRE on the morning before my oral defense—talk about timing. I improved my score by 11 points. I was over the threshold. I wanted to call dad, but there was no time. I quickly resubmitted a new application to the graduate school and rushed to my oral defense. I passed. Not with distinction, but passed, nonetheless. I walked my papers over to the Graduate School across the quad. It was a beautiful day. I called dad.

"Hey there, boy!" he answered as always.

"Hey, got some news."

"Yeah?"

"GRE score went up by 11 points."

"Hey, hey, there!" he said excitedly. "What about the comps?"

"Passed."

"Distinction?"

"Nah."

"Well, who gives a shit anyway," he said laughing.

I laughed. I was exhausted. I was proud. He was proud of me. I told him thanks for helping me pull through. He replied with something he had said to me many times before: "Bo, your greatest failures in life are those where you give up on yourself. Don't you ever sell yourself short."

Our Last Interaction

During his hospitalization, I spent countless nights attempting to keep up with coursework in desolate hospital cafeterias. I felt the pressure to publish and present, as any doctoral student desiring to work in academia does, but I knew that doing extra work would take time away from focusing on dad. Instead of working, I read about his illness in medical journals—a benefit of being a student. Dad got better, and he was sent home after multiple debriding procedures, followed by skin grafts to repair the damage from the NF. He recovered, moving from wheelchair to walker to a cane. We got in his truck a few times to let him drive around the neighborhood and to the grocery store, to regain a sense of normalcy. Everything was proceeding as it was supposed to.

One morning I awoke to the sound of him falling in the hallway outside my door. He was fine but had sprained his toe badly. This set into motion a series of complications which resulted in hospitalization and the amputation of half his right foot. He was distraught. Bouts of delirium in the hospital required him to be restrained. He would jerk at the straps and yell out, not knowing where he was. Sometimes he would forget who I was. Seeing him struggle was horrific. Little could be done to make him comfortable. Over time, his condition worsened. It all became too much for him to survive. He was not going to recover. My brother and I made the painful decision to place him in palliative care.

At this point, he had been unresponsive to stimuli for days. Staying with him in palliative care was exhausting. In the medical journals I read at night, I learned that in the moment of death, after breathing and heartbeat cease, the passive sense of hearing continues to function until the brain's oxygen supply is depleted. The one thing I could do in this time was to try to comfort him by telling him that he was loved, appreciated, and would be missed. My last interaction with my dad became a refrain in itself: slowing down chaos, territorializing my memory, and helping me to make sense of what was happening. I sincerely hoped the medical journals were right, and the refrain did the same for him.

Suddenly, his breathing pattern changed. We notified the nurse. She confirmed that he would die very soon. I held his hand tight. As he took those last labored breaths, I placed my palm on his forehead and stroked my thumb across it in the way that his mother—my grandmother—did when I was sick. Surely, she must have done the same decades ago when he was small. With tears streaming down my face, I repeated aloud what became a refrain that I still remember today,

"Everything is going to be ok, Daddy."

"I appreciate everything you've ever done for me."

"I love you, Daddy."

He took his last breath. I continued my refrain, finally settling on repeating the last line. I must have said, "I love you, Daddy" over a hundred times. It's funny how at 33-years-old, a son can still call their father *Daddy*. The man who had inspired me to live my life for me, who had always supported me, and who taught me to fight for what I wanted, was gone forever.

CONCLUSION

It's been 10 months now since Dad passed away. My brother and I frequently talk about Dad, recounting stories and laughing, going through pictures. The greatest pain is now the empty space he used to fill. I listen to his voicemails frequently. My favorite: "Hey Bo, it's your Dad. Just checking in. Give me a call. Love you, Son." Dad, I really wish I could.

I always thought theory was for academic work. I never thought it could help in real life, but it did. When first engaging in this project, postmodern theory clouded my memories. I wanted to claim his memory but felt like others' memories were delegitimizing my own. For all the confusion that is *ATP*, the concept of the refrain helped me to territorialize the memories of my dad and claim them as mine. But, like all refrains, they are meant to slow the chaos—not end or order it. As I grow older, I will change, and the world will change around me. These refrains will also change. I will come back to them, pick them up, examine them, evaluate them, and form new meaning. The refrains help me to remember.

REFERENCES

Abrams, L. (2010). *Oral history theory*. London, UK: Routledge.

Anderson, L., & Glass-Coffin, B. (2013). I learn by going: Autoethnographic modes of inquiry. In S. H. Jones, T. E. Adams, & C. Ellis (Eds.), *The handbook of autoethnography* (pp. 57–83). Walnut Creek, CA: Left Coast Press.

Deleuze, G., & Guattari, F. (1987). *A thousand plateaus: Capitalism and schizophrenia* (B. Massumi, Trans.). Minneapolis: University of Minnesota Press.

Ellis, C., & Bochner, A. P. (2000). Autoethnography, personal narrative, reflexivity: Researcher as subject. In N. K. Denzin & Y. S. Lincoln (Eds.), *The handbook of qualitative research* (pp. 733–768). Thousand Oaks, CA: Sage.

Feringa, M. (2019, April 21). After devastating truck accident, Auburn student uses faith to preserve through recovery. *The Auburn Plainsman*. Retrieved from https://www.theplainsman.com/article/2019/04/after-devastating-truck-accident-auburn-student-uses-faith-to-persevere-through-recovery.

Lincoln, Y. S. (1997). Self, subject, audience, text: Living at the edge, writing in the margins. In W. G. Tierney & Y. S. Lincoln (Eds.), *Representation and the text: Re-framing the narrative voice* (pp. 37–55). Albany: State University of New York Press.

Richardson, L. (1994). Writing: A method of inquiry. In N. K. Denzin & Y. S. Lincoln (Eds.), *Handbook of qualitative research* (pp. 516–529). Thousand Oaks, CA: Sage.

CHAPTER 9

I Can't Complain

Nancy Rankie Shelton

The degree to which I am conscious of my identity as an academic is relational to the amount of time that I spend with people not associated with university life. For me, this is usually time spent with my extended family. For, until this past year, I was the only Ph.D. among us. I've developed a habit of avoiding conversations on topics that I have studied, mainly because a typical verbal exchange becomes atypical, and I find myself either frustrated that other family members express themselves as education experts or because people stop listening to the points I am trying to make and move the conversation in an entirely different direction.

Last month, my niece, who recently earned her Ph.D., was part of a conversation that was directly related to her area of study. For the first time in my life, I was on the other side of a Ph.D.-informed conversation with my family. We were at her brother's home visiting him, his wife, and his three-month-old son when my niece commented that she wondered what this new generation of children felt like growing up in

N. R. Shelton (✉)
University of Maryland, Baltimore County, Baltimore, MD, USA
e-mail: nshelton@umbc.edu

© The Author(s) 2020
S. A. Shelton and N. Sieben (eds.),
Narratives of Hope and Grief in Higher Education,
https://doi.org/10.1007/978-3-030-42556-2_9

a world where they are constantly under surveillance—i.e., video baby monitors, cell phone cameras, and home security systems. The conversation moved into a discussion of cell phone use and screen time, to which I commented that we already know that there are cognitive changes in children, some even resulting in addictions to gaming, screen time, and the Internet. That naturally led to my sister commenting that since the introduction of television, some people have abused screen time by using the television as babysitters. This was when my niece commented that her dissertation work studied televisual narratives, and that her knowledge of how television generally affected societal change and individual cognitive growth could not be compacted into a casual family conversation. Her frustration with the conversation was evident to me. It silenced all of us.

In my silence, I reflected on my niece's reaction, on her choice not to share her expertise with us, and on my own past experiences with family members when I tried to share specialized knowledge. As a result of this reflection, I picked up my niece's dissertation and realized that even though my niece was not creating her life as a Ph.D. in a university setting, she is an academic. And as such, she struggled with living a perplexing dichotomy between who she is with family and who she is with collegial friends. This is similar to my own experiences.

This incident exemplified an approach to life that included a close connection to research and a studied approach to information sharing. Each of us sees the world through our own perspective, and my years connected to university life, academic research, and graduate-level teaching are strong parts of my identity. Therefore, when traumatic or life-changing events occur, it's natural for me to read published research to help me understand and adjust.

I am also a writer. I research writing and its contributions to children's cognitive growth. I teach writing pedagogy. I write with all my students, whether they are children or graduate students. I have many academic publications. I have many unpublished creative works. I have daybooks and diaries that hold a lifetime of artifacts, memories, and reflections.

Whether consciously or not, my identity is intricately entwined with my work as an academic. Therefore, when faced with the deepest grief imaginable, it was logical to turn to writing and research. This chapter elucidates the journey that I experienced weaving back and forth between grief, reading, writing, and being as I navigated my way into an entirely changed world.

An Emotional Ground Burst

On December 27, 2011, my husband suffered from a seizure. At the hospital that afternoon we were told that he had stage 4 metastatic cancer and an estimated 3–6 months to live. Jack lived for 5 months, thirteen days.

After Jack died, friends, colleagues, and family members supported my initial healing. They respected my sadness. Companionship was constant. Requests for help, whether home repairs or just opportunities for conversation, were granted. The people in my life were responsive and helpful. But after time, these supports waned.

A year after Jack's death, people's responses to me started to become dismissive. One family member commented, "You have to stop bringing your conversations back to you and Jack." A friend said, "Nancy, do you think you need to go to a counselor?" A colleague dismissed me with a wave of his hand, after he had asked me how I was doing. These verbal and nonverbal reactions felt like instant freezes.

I could not heal in those spaces. I doubted myself and questioned the progress that I knew I was making. I wondered if I should remove Jack's name from my vocabulary. I lost confidence in myself and lost balance in my life. I felt terribly vulnerable.

As a social constructivist and critical literacy scholar, I knew my identity was developed in part by the ways that people spoke to and about me, and that my reactions to such dialogue—first and third person—affected my thinking and behavior. I started to avoid people who sent strong negative messages, and to develop new friendships with people who didn't seem to mind if I kept Jack in my conversations. I continued to read and write as much as possible; I returned to my previous love of reviewing children's literature, not only because it was easier to comprehend, but also because the messages in the texts were often about the difficulties and joys of living. As I healed and was able to comprehend more complex texts again, I began a new path to understanding grief. I turned to the literature.

EMOTIONS AND COGNITION

Grief, similar to the concept of love, cannot hold up to a static definition that accurately describes the emotions that I felt. Grief is a multifaceted response to loss, with multiple domains that include, "feelings, psychological changes, impulses to action, and specific goal-oriented behavior" (Plutchik, 2001, p. 345). Various researchers have identified processes that a grieving person might work through, which are generalized as a result of studying many people. Plutchik explores the connection between emotions and evolutionary theory and addresses the difficulty of defining and studying emotions. He uses psychoevolutionary theory to unify various theoretical perspectives of human emotion. This was largely done through the evaluation of adaptive functions held by each emotion. Plutchik stated that "The function of emotion is to restore the individual to a state of equilibrium when unexpected or unusual events create disequilibrium" (p. 347).

Neimeyer (2010) explained a constructivist theory of bereavement as "grieving that entails an active effort to reaffirm or reconstruct a world of meaning that has been affected by loss" (p. 67). This approach allows survivors to adapt to life after loss. The success of the bereaved to make-sense of the loss directly connects with their ability to surmount disabling grief symptomatology. According to Neimeyer, "Constructivists recognize the innovative quality of all relationally responsive therapy, and accordingly view therapy as a process by which we join clients in articulating, symbolizing, and renegotiating those deeply personal meanings on which they rely to formulate their experience and action" (p. 88). This reformulation through reconstruction rather than relinquishing the relationship to the deceased is significant and negates the notion of *letting go*. Neimeyer suggests that forms of attachment that are uncontaminated by guilt and self-blame can play a central role in the grieving process.

The relief that I felt during and after reading theory and research related to grief began to answer my questions and address some of my wonderings. No, I should not take Jack out of my conversations. And avoiding people who sent me negative messages was the right thing to do. My evolving understanding of emotions, especially grief, led me to question the multiple cultural expressions of grief in our society.

In old western movies, which my mother and I enjoyed throughout my childhood, widows wore black for a year. All my life people around me shared insight to family and friends during times of loss, sharing clichés like: "The first year is the hardest," "You'll get through this," or "God will help you through." As a new widow, I was told not to make any important decisions for a year. These experiences led me to believe that I would heal significantly during the first year; that there was some definable space to get through, as if I might emerge out of grief through a proverbial doorway and enter into a space much like my previous life, just without Jack present.

Weaving a Path Through a Changed World

Fortunately, I was faculty in a department chaired by a man who showed compassion during my cancer-and-death journey with Jack. I went on family leave immediately, first for a semester and then for another, using my accrued sick leave to ensure continuous income. I was also on schedule for a sabbatical, which I applied for and was granted, thus giving me a full calendar year after Jack's death to resume full duties. During the 2012–2013 academic year, I focused on research and writing. I was co-directing a major research project and had signed a contract with Routledge Press just days before Jack's health changed the direction of my life. The project investigated the impact of literacy policy on current teaching and learning.

It was extremely difficult to continue this work because the politics of literacy put me into a state of agitation. In the past, conversations with Jack would bridge my work and a peaceful life. Those conversations were now impossible, and for the months that my colleagues and I wrote up our research, I lived in a constant state of tension. But the work had to be done; I was co-leading a team of researchers who were relying on the publication for their own professional advancements. Over and over, I would return to Plutchik's (2001) work and remind myself that, "feelings do not happen in isolation. They are responses to significant situations in an individual's life, and often they motivate actions" (p. 346). I used this theory as a motivator to fulfill my professional obligation to my co-researchers.

Personal Challenges: Becoming Single

A grieving person is an individual. Her responses are unique. Her circumstances are personal. My early conceptualization that I might eventually settle into a life that was somewhat similar to the life Jack and I shared continued to be a goal for me. However, the impossibility of reaching this goal was becoming strikingly clear as I struggled to adjust to my loss. Having a male partner was a privilege that in ways protected me from being devalued and disrespected; I had quite suddenly become a single woman who was no longer safe from of other men who would be inclined to "take advantage" of my perceived vulnerabilities. The assumption is that woman alone cannot hit back or push back in the ways that my husband could have—because of male privilege. So I became an easy target for the effects of gender inequality. I experienced many incidences of exposed vulnerability that included sexual harassment, building contractors trying to take advantage of me, and violent verbal and physical threats made by a neighbor. More lugubrious than any other was when the reality of wage disparity between men and women hit home. I had suddenly become responsible for all family expenses—expenses that had once been paid with two incomes.

Emotional challenges related to the loss of one's partner are compounded by the realities of managing financially. Again, I approached this problem using knowledge. When it became nearly impossible to pay my bills, I started wondering how other people with whom I worked seemed very financially sound. I began researching publicly available salary information, as well as current practices that attempt to equalize employment compensation and opportunities for all. What I found was both disturbing and motivating. I could only understand my world by writing. So I did.

Illusions of Equity

I read history as if
  milestones have been met
Mary Mallon
  exiled, labeled
Lucretia Mott
  abolitionist, suffragist
Clara Lemlich
  Women's Labor Organizer

I read as if women
  have attained equal status
as if women
  are respected in the workplace
as if women
  are now valued the way society
Values Men

with equally shared
  positions of power
with non-discriminating
  paychecks
with civil
    rights

Then reality awakens
  and
I remember
  being bullied by
male teachers
    sixth grade, ninth grade, tenth grade
I remember
  being groped
  when I was so young
  my sexuality lie dormant

And yet, I lived with hope
  when Congress passed
  the Equal Rights Amendment
learning by watching
  other women, using
  their example, taking
  action, believing
things would be different
  if I became educated
  and competed fairly in the world

Focusing on my studies
  hurrying to a college
    education   Working
    any job to save for tuition

Matriculating
  I made it! Yet
    I can't remember
    other females in
      my math classes
      female professors
      leading any classes
    I do remember
      swimming in a
      sea of men

Naively thinking it would be different
    if I moved
    to the state capital
    where our laws were made
    to protect *all* people
  and then

I remember my history there
  being turned down for a job
    because boys
    need role models
  being followed by a carload of men
    while walking home from
    the only job I could
    get: volunteering

Refusing to retreat
  after I earned my degree
  moving again
to a place
even farther from my roots
Again I remember...
  My fill-in job as a waitress
    while I searched
    and searched
      and searched
    for a professional appointment
      where the male chef
        intimidated female waitresses
        with foul language

sexual overtures
and threatening gestures

I thought it would be different
if the restaurant owner
knew what was happening
to his female employees
but then
I remember
 being propositioned
 by that filthy pervert
  and crying when I
  told my father that
  more men should
  be as honorable as he

I watched the
Equal Rights Amendment
Stagnate
Two states short
Of Ratification

Still, I believed in
 Meritocracy
 that Education
 would set me Free
 eventually delivering Respect

Positive things could be different
 I earned my Master's Degree
 joining the legions of
 teachers who
 educate the citizenry
 but then

I remember
 Teaching is an
 underpaid profession
 dominated by women

I kept seeking
 hunting
  believing
 The difference I sought
 had to be somewhere

Relentlessly studying
elevating to the professoriate
    only to find myself earning
    tens of thousands of dollars
    less than my male peers
at a university that
publicly brags about its
    diversity
and equality
    policies
whose attorney lets my pleas
for fair salary
sit unanswered for months
    and months
        and months
            and months

While I try to balance a budget
    that would be
    so easily satisfied
    if only I had been
        Born Male

Now I understand what is different.
    I am female.

The Equal Rights Amendment
    Languishes
Despite extended deadlines,
    marches, hunger strikes
    civil disobedience
    Grace Hopper
    Virginia Apgar
    Marie Maynard Daly
    Rosalyn Sussmen Yalow
Women who, I guess,
    don't deserve
    Equal Rights in
    the country they
    Serve

I'm too tired
    to keep fighting
    but I must if
    I want to make that difference
My official letter from EEOC

admits to thousands of cases
all waiting for attention
while so many

        dreams

            linger in limbo

And I know I must
double each female's
respect quotient
to equal one male's

I feel like the
        little rubber ball
tethered to the end
        of a thin but strong
elastic thread
        beaten again
and again
        and again
by the paddle
        attached to it
Never set free
        beyond the boundaries
allowed by the
        measured distance
of the men who
        designed this game

A game
  I no longer
    believe
      will ever end

        My
                illusions
                    of equity
                        have faded
                            away

Although my financial challenges continued, for a time just taking procedural and professional action to equalize my salary helped to keep me focused and fighting for women's rights.

Renewed Research Focus

In academia, faculty responsibilities fall into three domains: service, teaching, and research. Because the book publication (Shelton & Altwerger, 2015) marked the conclusion of a major research project, a natural shift occurred when I returned to full-time duties for the following the 2013–2014 academic year. My professional efforts were channeled into: *service*, rebuilding the education department's children's literature collection, which required reading and reviewing current, award-winning children's books; *teaching*, updating my syllabi; and shifting my *research* interests to writing my memoir.

The day of Jack's seizure, my sister had advised me to write everything down that the medical staff shared with me, because I would need the notes for reference. She was right; I did need them to keep up with the constantly changing diagnosis and treatment. However, I also used the legal pad and my laptop to record copious notes, personal thoughts, and responses, including comments about our environment and conversations with Jack and others. Very early on in Jack's journey, I knew that one day I would use the information to write a book. Though I could give this part of my notetaking no real academic energy at that time, I did collect everything. When the time came, I had all the data that I needed.

I took the same approach to writing my memoir as I had with qualitative research projects that I had conducted. My data set included:

- documents, notes, medical information provided by all medical staff;
- continuous time-coded notes capturing everything said and done;
- daily transcriptions of the hand-written notes with added reflections or events that occurred later in the day relevant to the what was captured in writing. I reviewed medical documents and compared them to my notes to make sure I had an accurate understanding of Jack's diagnosis and treatment;
- photo documentation; and
- reflective essays capturing events/feelings.

I organized my data and created online files. A manuscript started to take shape in my mind. It didn't take long before I had envisioned the project and could begin writing. Though a memoir is a story, technically it is a work of nonfiction; I had all the needed documentation, but I struggled to emerge from a rather dull diary-like chronological account of Jack's and my experiences.

In November 2013, a colleague and I organized a writing retreat for University of Maryland, Baltimore County (UMBC) faculty that afforded sustained time to write with feedback from another writer. During that retreat, I worked with an introductory chapter of my memoir. As it turned out, one of the participating professors, Diane, was also a widow, and she was a cancer patient. Diane's interest and feedback were genuine. The questions that she asked and suggestions that she made during our peer conferences gave me both insights and confidence as a writer.

Writing and sharing that first chapter was invigorating. It was the turning point of my journey to regain my momentum as an academic, by somehow merging my personal and professional selves. My writing, whether personal or academic, is always fueled by reading. My ongoing service and teaching work were slowly sharing energy with my writing. I knew that I would definitely abandon the line of research that made my blood boil—politics of literacy—and energize myself as a different sort of writer: one who grounds her work in lived experiences but writes for a non-academic audience.

Renewed Teaching/Service Focus

As an elementary teacher, and now an educator's educator, my students and I explore multiple topics through children's literature. Rebuilding the department library required the department to purchase currently published award-winning books, all of which I read. In addition, I returned to my practice of emptying the public library shelves of all newly released children's literature. I read constantly. It was mesmerizing to hear authors' voices describe death in ways that I understood but that family, friends, and colleagues did not. I read as Galante's character Jack described his father's experience: "It was like he had extra arms or something and just carried everything for as long as he could. And then, when Mom died, he kind of let go, I guess" (2017, p. 86), and I felt the weight of caring for Jack, and how I felt the morning that he died. I analyzed how the central theme that drove Benjamin's *The Thing About Jellyfish* (2015) plot was how Suzy, the main character, came to terms with her friend's death; I realized that it mirrored the central theme in my own life: I had to come to terms with Jack's death. I felt the healing powers of literature in Pearsall's (2008) characters' determination to realistically better their current situations. The experiences in the children's books spoke to me as an adult. I kept reading and re-reading. I organized book talks with students and colleagues, listening carefully to everyone's responses.

In the texts above, as with most books, I identified multiple themes that included many experiences and realities present in our society. While I personally felt the discussions related to death, which also propelled my writing, the many other themes—e.g., friendship, ADHD, coming of age, Tourette's syndrome, cultural differences, selective mutism, financial stability, LGBTQIA—were of equal importance in terms of a teacher's understanding, as well as inclusion in a diverse literature collection. Eventually, I turned this part of my teaching and service work into my next research project.

The predominance of teachers who are not well-equipped to teach students from diverse backgrounds demands attention to multicultural teaching pedagogy (Banks & Banks, 2015). In response to this need, a colleague and I began developing a curriculum designed to prepare preservice teachers to meet the needs of children in our changing society. The curriculum includes nonfiction classroom vignettes, written responses to the vignettes, and authentic small group discussions. Class discussions informed by exemplary children's literature follow. The literature, appropriate for classrooms, helps teachers to understand and to teach children who are homeless, whose parents are incarcerated, who are gender nonconforming, who live in violent neighborhoods, or have recently lost a family member or friend to death.

Children's Literature

Children suffer loss; they are exposed to death; they lose loved ones as a result of illness, accidents, and violence. When children live with emotional stress, we do not need to teach them Plutchik and Neimeyer's theories but can help them to find comfort, compassion, and understanding by helping them reconstruct an identity necessary for healthy healing. We can be companions in their grief, we can share children's literature that connects to their feelings, and we can give them hope that healing does come. We can help children and young adults realize that healing is individual, and not scripted behaviors or processes that just unfold over time.

There are many exemplary books that realistically introduce death, that range in audience from preschoolers (Parr, 2015) to those written for young adults, such as Cummings' (2004) *Red Kayak*. In Cummings' story, eighth-grade characters face the consequences of a prank that causes a child's death. Numerous children's novels mimic Neimeyer's constructivist approach to grief recovery and address how children cope with grief. In *The Memory String* (Bunting & Rand, 2000), a child used her late mother's necklace to stay connected to her mother and worked through difficult life changes that included her efforts to see herself with a new identity as a step-daughter. *The Thing About Jellyfish* (Benjamin, 2015), mentioned earlier, and *Dirt* (Orenstein, 2017) allow readers to understand the psychological changes that occur as a result of grief (Plutchik, 2001). In *Mrs. Bixby's Last Day*, Anderson (2016) cleverly wove humor and sensitivity throughout the text, which exemplifies "impulses to action" as a response to loss. In Mosier's (2017) *Train I Ride*, a twelve-year-old whose grandmother died must spend three days on a train traveling from Los Angeles to Chicago to live with an uncle she'd never met, revealing the intensity of how relationships change as a result of death. However, I think of all the messages in the children's books, my favorite always came down to the authors who honored the time that it took for the characters to find some semblance of normality, most especially Davis's (2017) *Superstar*, which took place 5 years after Lester's father's death.

CONCLUSION

The multiple life challenges present in the various children's literature books constantly reminded me of Jack's source of strength. During all stages of his treatment, we saw children undergoing care for catastrophic illnesses. Jack would turn to me and say, "That's why I can't complain." I have used and continue to use his strength. With the help of others, including Plutchik and Neimeyer, I navigate my emotions and actions in ways that keep me moving forward. In a sense, it is moving *through*, but I now know that I'm not moving to some revision of my previous life. I have built a new life, one that fits the people and resources available to me.

During this journey, many parts of my life have changed. My work in higher education continued but since my memoir was published (Shelton, 2016), my reading and writing have been both academic and non-academic. My appeal to the university to equalize salaries went as far as I could take it, and I eventually reached an agreement with the university administration that increased my compensation but, unfortunately, fell short of stimulating university-wide policy change. I continued to develop curriculum for teachers; I promoted children's literature as one of the most important influences in a child's life; and I continued to turn to scholarly voices to learn and understand my ever-changing world.

REFERENCES

Anderson, J. D. (2016). *Ms. Bixby's last day*. New York, NY: Walden Pond Press.

Banks, J. A., & Banks, C. A. (2015). *Multicultural education: Issues and perspectives* (9th ed.). Hoboken, NJ: Wiley.

Benjamin, A. (2015). *The thing about jellyfish: A novel*. New York, NY: Little, Brown.

Bunting, E., & Rand, T. (2000). *The memory string*. New York, NY: Clarion Books.

Cummings, P. (2004). *Red kayak*. New York, NY: Puffin Books.

Davis, M. (2017). *Superstar*. New York, NY: Harper.

Galante, C. (2017). *Stealing our way home*. New York, NY: Scholastic Press.

Mosier, P. (2017). *Train I ride* (1st ed.). New York, NY: Harper.

Neimeyer, R. (2010). Reconstructing the continuing bond: A constructivist approach to grief therapy. In *Studies in meaning 4: Constructivist perspectives on theory, practice and social justice* (pp. 65–91). New York, NY: Pace University Press.

Orenstein, D. G. (2017). *Dirt*. New York, NY: Scholastic Press.

Parr, T. (2015). *The goodbye book*. New York, NY: Little, Brown.

Pearsall, S. (2008). *All of the above*. New York, NY: Little, Brown.

Plutchik, R. (2001). The nature of emotions: Human emotions have deep evolutionary roots, a fact that may explain their complexity and provide tools for clinical practice. *American Scientist, 89*(4), 344–350.

Shelton, N. R. (2016). *5-13: A memoir of love, loss and survival*. New York, NY: Garn Press.

Shelton, N. R., & Altwerger, B. (Eds.). (2015). *Literacy policies and practices in conflict: Reclaiming classrooms in networked times*. New York, NY: Routledge.

PART III

Humanizing Grief in Politicized Moments

CHAPTER 10

I Refuse to Be a Bystander

Crystal L. Beach

To be quite honest, it's hard to keep up with the number of school shootings we have been faced with here in the United States, even though
we constantly are reminded of just how many there are (Ahmed, 2018;
Everytown, 2019). After all, in just the first 19 weeks in 2019, there
were 15 school shootings—almost a shooting per week (Lou & Walker,
2019). I've wondered if the reason I feel desensitized to these numbers is
thanks to the prolific news coverage of events, to the conversations with
people who claim it could never happen in their communities, or to the
sad reality that shootings do happen far too often in the most unlikely
places—like schools.

As a high school English language arts (ELA) teacher, I think about
the worst possible scenario every day, and no, that's not an exaggeration.
Is it morbid? Maybe, but it is the reality in which I live. As my students
and I examine authors and their works, I remind them that everyone has
a story to tell, including teachers and students. And I think it's important
to consider the experiences that shape us as teachers, especially because
those experiences ultimately define what we value and what we bring into
our philosophies of teaching.

C. L. Beach (✉)
Union County Schools, Blairsville, GA, USA

© The Author(s) 2020
S. A. Shelton and N. Sieben (eds.),
Narratives of Hope and Grief in Higher Education,
https://doi.org/10.1007/978-3-030-42556-2_10

See, I've lived through the unimaginable: April 16, 2007. While it may seem like a random date to many, it's one that will forever be ingrained in every ounce of my being. On that day, I was a student at Virginia Tech when we experienced one of the "deadliest shooting rampages in US history" (CNN Library, 2018). My memories of that day still bring overwhelming feelings of grief in ways that I can't explain.

However, faced with the harsh reality that many want teachers armed (Heim, 2018), and active shooter simulation trainings and conversations are becoming standard professional development in both secondary and higher education, it's no wonder that the worst possible scenarios pervade my thoughts. Yet, I decided long ago that I refuse to be a bystander or a victim to the grief that gun violence has brought to me.

Thus, this chapter looks to explore how my lived experience with gun violence in schools has shaped me into the person, and subsequently, the teacher I am today. It will highlight how I continue to try to navigate through my grief by focusing on building a justice-oriented classroom for all of my students, where our reading and writing play huge roles in building our classroom community.

April 16, 2007

Spring in Blacksburg, Virginia is all about flipping a coin to determine if you will be wearing shorts and a t-shirt as you feel like you sweated 10 lbs. off walking across campus, or if you will be wrapped up in the warmest clothing you have as the wind off the mountains blows across the Drillfield and snow flurries cling to your eyelashes. April 16 was a cold day, and bundled up for my walk, I cursed under my breath as frigid gusts of air hit me in the face.

On my hike across the Drillfield that morning, I thought it was strange to see a police car go flying up onto a curb. "What's his deal?" I thought. I hurried to my building, too cold to realize that he was probably the first responder on the scene of what would turn into one of the worst days of my life.

Nearing the building, I saw people standing at the glass doors, eyes wide and filled with panic and absolute fear. I didn't know what to think as they frantically motioned and yelled for me to *run* to the building. The heavy door slammed as I rushed in, and they wrapped a huge chain around the door handles. "Where in the world did they find that thing?"

I remember thinking, rather than questioning why they were locking us in so aggressively.

That's when I heard the news: "There's a shooter on campus! Everything is shut down... We're supposed to stay hidden and out of sight...already one death confirmed..."

I stood there stunned. I blinked. They had to be mistaken. And so I did what every person was *trying* to do: I pulled out my cell phone to call my mom. It wouldn't connect. "What the hell?" I reached for the landline in my office as someone yelled for me to "Get down and take cover *NOW!*"

I snatched the phone from the corner desk and, crouching underneath the desk, dialed my mom at work. She worked at our hometown's health department and was in-and-out with patients most days, but thankfully on this day, she picked up. "Mom, can you turn on the news? I think something has happened here," I said.

"What do you mean something has happened? What are you talking about?"

I replied, "I don't know. We are on lockdown. I've gotta go, but please check. Mom, I just want to come home." Tears welled in my eyes, and I hung up the phone with the promise that I would call her back.

Next, I tried to text my softball teammates and friends, but nothing would go through. Then, I tried emailing. A friend across campus said he'd seen a lot of police cars, but then our correspondence locked up, as even the Internet moved in slow motion. I peeked around the corner and moved into the office where everyone was quietly huddled around a TV. Reports of multiple shooting victims. And the number of victims continued climbing—this has to be a mistake.

We were finally given the "All Clear!" as officers officially searched and cleared our building late that afternoon. We were allowed to leave ... only to sit in traffic around campus as news vans packed into parking lots. "How did this happen?" I cried, as I slowly made my way off campus.

Later, I would learn that 32 of our own lost their lives far too soon. I would sit around with my teammates on the wooden steps of their apartment complex, Collegiate Suites, as we waited to hear the names: names of friends gone forever. We would learn that our softball teammate had barely survived inside her classroom—in the *single* room not breached. We would learn all of the terrible details of what took place that day. I thought back to seeing the shooter's face, one I saw often around Shanks Hall, and wondered how he could bring such hate to this place and these people, loved so deeply by so many. We watched our lives paraded on the flurry of news channels. We walked to and from the candlelight vigils with arms linked. We cried. I would turn and cry into my ever-loyal and loving dog, Dane, who curled up next to me, understanding that I just couldn't move off the sofa for our daily walk. My former teammate and best-friend-who-is-really-family arrived immediately from California. We would listen to Nikki Giovanni's (2007) wise words: "We will prevail, We will prevail, We WILL prevail, We ARE Virginia Tech."

I've been back to Virginia Tech many times since graduating; it's truly one of my most cherished places. I walk the memorial site every time I visit, honoring those 32 lives gone too soon. I still cry, especially when I hear of another senseless school shooting where communities are affected forever. No one should have to feel that pain. So many years ago, yet it feels just like yesterday.

Today, I am a high school ELA teacher-researcher and coach. I get to work with incredible young people every day. However, not a day goes by that I don't consider "What If?" And as a teacher, I'm an avid believer in professional development (PD) because I strive to be the best that I can be for my students; PD is something I truly value. However, I never imagined that PD would include me re-living what it was like at Virginia Tech. I guess this is the reality in which so many of us live in today.

TEACHER PROFESSIONAL DEVELOPMENT: ACTIVE SHOOTER SIMULATION

At my previous high school, I was lucky to have a few great departmental colleagues who were also great friends. We made every day an adventure and found fun in the most mundane of meetings or PD.

One night I had reached my limit with grading a stack of essays. "These papers can wait for now." I rubbed my tired eyes and texted two of my friends from work to see what they were doing. "Come get food with us!" and just like that, I was out the door. Nothing beats good food with great friends, who also happen to understand what 150 essays feel like to grade.

As we sat together sharing laughs, someone brought up our PD, and an awkward silence took over the table. "So, have you heard about what we are doing?"

I looked around and shook my head no. "Something with school safety, right?"

More worried looks. "Um, from what I heard, we are having an active shooter simulation." Silence.

"What do you mean? *Safety* and *simulation* are two very different words." They all agreed, and I immediately texted two of our assistant principals. Yes, on a Saturday night at 9:30 PM, I was texting about work, but I felt the panic settling in my chest.

Their responses confirmed that we were having some sort of simulation training with local law enforcement. Aware of my experiences, my assistant principals both told me that they would let me know exactly what PD entailed, and that I was welcome to sit out the entire training. The next day felt like forever, as I waited to learn what the simulation involved.

PD day arrived, and we were sitting in the cafeteria enjoying a catered meal. However, I quickly realized I was in trouble. A colleague entered the room and, looking at me with wide eyes, asked if I was going to be ok. I laughed and said, "Of course!" in a tone too loud to cover up my anxiety. And that's when the Police SWAT team walked in with their weapons drawn, surveying the area.

From there, we were divided into groups to act out scenarios with the training team. Some colleagues were *excited* to play the bad guy. Some colleagues were in awe of the SWAT team and snapping pictures to post on social media. Some colleagues couldn't care less. Some colleagues looked at me, knowing how difficult it was for me. And I walked down the hall, to play simulation, trying to hold myself together; after all, I was *tough*. Tough people don't just leave or quit, even when they can feel tears in the corners of their eyes—they blame them on allergies.

I ended up walking into the athletic team meeting room, where a small group of colleagues and I seemed to be forgotten by the scenarios happening throughout the building. No one from the SWAT team came into our room—yet. Some knew about my experience at Virginia Tech and were shocked that I was even there for that PD. When SWAT finally came into our room to practice their search, I couldn't help but think, "That's not really what they look like when they're clearing the room." Been there; done that.

When I became a teacher, I never thought PD would include active shooter simulations. And while I believe that we need to have important conversations about school safety improvements, I can only pray that if the worst ever happens, I can hold that door long enough to save my students. Or that he—yes, "he" because we know the demographic of school shooters in the United States (Cai & Patel, 2019), even though many want to ignore those conversations—is killed or kills himself before he makes it to my floor. These thoughts were my takeaway from active shooter simulation PD. I didn't need a simulation to know what I would need to do if the worst ever happened to me again.

TEACHER PROFESSIONAL DEVELOPMENT: EMERGENCY RESPONSES

As more school shootings headline the news, school safety continues to be an important focal point nationwide. I do think that it is important for schools to work closely with local law enforcement to ensure that schools are using best practices and procedures to protect their campuses. Schools are supposed to be safe spaces, which includes having honest conversations with teachers and students about safety measures.

For this reason, it was no surprise that after the previous active shooter simulation PD, we had state law enforcement officers come speak to us about emergency responses the following year. But really, it was "Active Shooter Training." I knew that I was in trouble when the speaker said that he was going to break down some of the bigger shootings and help us understand what went wrong in each of them.

First came the data in pie charts. I nervously laughed and whispered to my friends, "Here we go!" Next came a slide with headlines of news stories. I began to feel my chest fill with anxiety again. And then there was Virginia Tech. I'll be honest: I was so shocked and unprepared for this presentation that I was stunned at the presented information. I wanted to yell, "YOU DON'T KNOW WHAT YOU'RE TALKING ABOUT!" I wanted to run out. But I'm tough, remember? So I sat there feeling like I was about to explode, boiling up like a teapot left on the burner for too long.

As the speaker started to detail each room at Virginia Tech, labeling victims' actions as "success" or "failure," I began to see the faces of those lost. They weren't just marks of success or failure on some safety sheet for me. It was like I was reliving the moment, sitting on those wooden stairs with my teammates as we learned of those we had lost in those rooms. The last thing that I heard was the speaker talking about the *teacher who held the door*. The tears flooded down my face. That *teacher who held the door* came unbidden to my mind; I saw Holocaust survivor and professor Liviu Librescu's kind eyes. I walked out.

My phone quickly filled with texts from colleagues and my assistant principals, who apologized that they had no idea what the presentation's scope would be. They blamed themselves for not asking more questions. One colleague ran outside after me, all the way out to my car and hugged me tightly, making sure that I was okay. Luckily, I only lived five minutes from my school, so I was able to rush home and regroup. I was so ashamed that I had walked out, and even more ashamed I had cried—and in front people! I kept wondering how this must look for someone who'd considered being an administrator one day. "How can you be so weak?" I thought to myself.

After talking with my teammates and drinking an unsweetened green tea—that always seems to make things better—I headed back to my classroom. I hoped to arrive before everyone else, to hide my very swollen, red, splotchy face. I kept the lights off and the door barely cracked. It was then that my dear friend and science teacher extraordinaire came to check on me. I teared up again and admitted my embarrassment of not being able to control my emotions. Her words still stick with me today: "Crystal, it's okay to feel something. You have to allow yourself to feel." And that's when I thought to myself that I didn't become a teacher to not feel. I can't teach and care for kids if I don't feel. I can't teach kids to empathize with the world around them if I can't feel. After all, I became a teacher to create change and empower young people with the hope of creating a better tomorrow.

BUILDING A COMMUNITY OF HOPE

It's hard to go to work every day and recognize the possibility of a school shooting. It's not that I *try* to think about it; it is my reality. However, please understand that my experience at Virginia Tech has not consumed me; instead, it's motivated me to teach kindness and compassion every day. It would be easy to be a bystander in my grief, but I refuse. Instead, I focus on supporting my students through their moments of darkness, encouraging my students as they share their own stories and read about others' experiences. I do tough work with amazing colleagues who value justice-oriented teaching practices, to ensure that all students are safe and valued. It is through these activities that together we create a community of hope in my classroom and beyond.

Turning Darkness into Light

I recently wrote about a time in which I felt I failed my students early in my career: one of their peers had died unexpectedly. However, my students taught me to find hope in that grief and failure. I reflected,

> It was one of those days when you needed a reminder of why you do what you do. (Every teacher, no matter how long we've been teaching, knows what I'm talking about!) A Twitter notification pops up on my phone, and I head to see what was there. To my utter shock, I watched a video my student was a part of for the #ThankYouTeachers initiative (https://twitter.com/seminoles/status/920776567969714176). In it, she references the writing assignment I had my students do that devastating day years ago—a day when I felt that I failed them in so many ways. She talks about how I inspired her, and all I could think about was how much she and her peers inspired me. This is what teaching is all about to me: inspiring others to be their best selves even through the darkest times. (Beach, 2019)

Talk about a jaw dropping moment that is one of the most moving of my career. It's something that I always share when I'm mentoring teachers: never forget how much of an impact you can have on your students *and*, perhaps more importantly, how much you can learn from them as they influence your life, too.

So, of course we write in my classroom; it is an ELA class after all. However, we write in ways that surpass any performance goals or state standards. We write to experience the world around us and to share our worlds with others. We write in remembrance of those we have lost and to leave legacies for future generations. And those are the stories that matter most in my classroom.

OUR STORIES MATTER

I feel that if we are really going to focus on making schools *safe*, then we can't be remiss to acknowledge that for many students, school has never been a *safe* place for learning due to a variety of issues that include discrimination (Jones, 2019) or language learning. For this reason, another way I try to support my students is by acknowledging their home literacies by helping them find stories that resonate or help them to build compassion for others.

For example, I try to create socially just classroom learning experiences for my students by reminding them that they have a *right* to their own language(s). Through writing portfolios, book trailers, public service announcements, and various other digital literacy practices, students are able to show their learning through a variety of language(s) and modes of communication. After all, "we must remember that our job is never 'just' teaching, but *just* teaching to ensure that all students' voices are heard and valued through justice-oriented literacy learning that remembers the past, acknowledges the present, and believes in the future" (Beach, Falter, & Jones, 2019, p. 51).

In addition, while we have our common texts from the bookroom, my students bring in current events related to tough issues that affect them; we even share book, movie, and TV show titles. There are some ELA teachers who scoff at young adult literature or Netflix series in classrooms, but I believe that to be a justice-oriented teacher, my job is to help connect kids with texts that speak to them and their experiences. And sometimes that means taking suggestions from students. So when a student suggested I read Marieke Nijkamp's (2018) book *This Is Where It Ends*, I went and picked it up from my local bookstore. I'm not ready to read the main part of the book—even now as I write this—but I have read the author's note in the back. Nijkamp (2018) wrote:

> I didn't understand how the possibility of death and fear of violence could be an almost accepted part of education. I knew and know it's not always avoidable. I lived with death for a long time, and I understand the fear of violence as well. But I wondered: Could this not be avoided? Should this not be avoided? (p. 288)

Nijkamp's words resonated for the student too—because it connected to her concerns on school violence, which she brought up in class. It's through these stories—fictional or not—that we learn from others' experiences and/or realize we aren't alone. And though we share stories together that help negotiate tough issues, it is important to acknowledge that our profession still has a lot of work to do to provide the guidance that our students deserve.

There Is Work to Do

While a focus on school safety is important, and creating a justice-oriented classroom, too, it's also just as important to consider the communities in which our students live. Despite the fact that many people assumed students at my previous school had the *good life* because of their successes in academics, athletics, and the arts, not all were affluent, and affluence doesn't mean one doesn't face hardships when they leave school every day. I know that my students come from all walks of life and have a myriad of experiences that they bring with them when they walk into my classroom. And I cannot ignore that many of them have been victims to gun violence and community violence. However, they, too, choose not to be bystanders to their grief.

In my own continuing efforts to actively work through grief, particularly grief over gun violence, I chose to serve as a member of the National Council of Teachers of English's (NCTE) Committee Against Racism and Bias in the Teaching of English. This decision was based on the ways that I have come to recognize gun violence as inextricably linked to racism. I was honored to co-write a post with my colleagues that included resources to help teachers and schools have tough conversations about gun violence and race. We wrote,

> The intersection of gun violence and racism in schools is a conversation that may be new to some NCTE members, but it is not new in many communities of color, where students have been engaging in these conversations for decades, seeking justice and demanding change. (NCTE's Committee, 2018)

I am reminded that I can't ignore the issues that our students face, especially within communities of color, and I believe as teachers, we must be sure that we are committed to addressing them directly.

In addition, the committee drafted a Resolution that we delivered at the 2018 NCTE Annual Convention, which focused on the magnified and misguided efforts to bring guns into schools to prevent school shootings. Our belief is that educators have an essential role in sustaining non-violence in the face of conflict, which means that teachers need trauma-informed care education, crisis counselors, support for mental health in all schools, and opportunities to include diverse representations from community members, including students, to join school safety discussions (Dredger et al., 2018). Again, I believe that we cannot forget the fact that many of our students are affected in some way by gun violence every day. There is much work to do *together* to ensure that we are advocating for our students and supporting them as they advocate for themselves, too.

#neVerforgeT

As a college student, I never thought that my school would be remembered as one of the United States's worst mass shootings. As a teacher, I never imagined I'd be involved with active shooter stimulations or emergency response training. However, both are sad realities.

Yet, I refuse to be a bystander to my grief because my students are too important to me. Because no one should ever have to live through what we did at Virginia Tech, and because we know through writing and reading stories that we find communities of hope. We remember (Virginia Tech, 2018) in order to create a better future together. Even though there is much work to be done, teachers, students, and school communities remind me every day that the future is bright, and I am hopeful we can *all* influence positive changes. Though perhaps cliché, I tell my students every day as they leave my room: "Go be kind to someone. Go make someone smile. Go do something great in the world today!" They know that I really mean it.

References

Ahmed, S. (2018, May 25). There has been, on average, 1 school shooting every week this year. *CNN*. Retrieved from https://www.cnn.com/2018/03/02/us/school-shootings-2018-list-trnd/index.html.

Beach, C. L. (2019). Turning darkness into light: Opportunities to build community and learn from our students. In N. Thompson & K. Jones (Eds.), *The teacher casebook*. Retrieved from https://www.teachercasebook.com/casebook/turning-darkness-into-light-opportunities-to-build-community-and-learn-from-our-students.

Beach, C. L., Falter, M. M., & Jones, S. P. (2019). "Just" teaching: (Re)imagining our students' right to their own language through digital literacies. *Arkansas English Journal, 4*(1), 44–53.

Cai, W., & Patel, J. K. (2019, May 11). A half-century of school shootings like Columbine, Sandy Hook and Parkland. *The New York Times*. Retrieved from https://www.nytimes.com/interactive/2019/05/11/us/school-shootings-united-states.html.

CNN Library. (2018, May 2). Virginia Tech shootings fast facts. *CNN*. Retrieved from https://www.cnn.com/2013/10/31/us/virginia-tech-shootings-fast-facts/index.html.

Dredger, K. (Chair.), Baca, D., Beach, C. L., Falter, M., German, L., Gorham, R, ... Yurko, K.: The Committee Against Racism and Bias in the Teaching of English. (2018, November). *Resolution on alternatives to guns in schools.* Presented at NCTE Annual Convention, Houston, TX.

Everytown. (2019). *Everytown for gun safety.* Retrieved from https://everytown.org.

FSU Seminoles [Seminoles]. (2017, October 18). "She gave me the passion for English and education."—Tessa Daniels Shoutout to Dr. Beach! @CFPExtraYard #CFPExtraYard" [Tweet]. Retrieved from https://twitter.com/seminoles/status/920776567969714176.

Giovanni, N. (2007, April 17). *Convocation address.* Retrieved from https://www.remembrance.vt.edu/2007/archive/giovanni_transcript.html.

Heim, J. (2018, May 3). Across the country, measures to arm teachers in schools stall. *Washington Post*. Retrieved from https://www.washingtonpost.com/local/education/across-the-country-measures-to-arm-teachers-in-schools-stall/2018/05/03/7ef6193a-4193-11e8-8569-26fda6b404c7_story.html?noredirect=on&utm_term=.808_efa8a2f23.

Jones, S. P. (2019, November). Mapping racial trauma in schools [Facebook video post]. Retrieved from https://www.facebook.com/mappingracialtrauma/videos/337601433476667/.

Lou, M., & Walker, C. (2019, May 9). There have been 15 school shootings in the US so far this year. *CNN*. Retrieved from https://www.cnn.com/2019/05/08/us/school-shootings-us-2019-trnd/index.html.

NCTE's Committee Against Racism and Bias in the Teaching of English. (2018, April). Intersection of race and guns in schools: Resources for teaching in these times. *NCTE*. Retrieved from http://www2.ncte.org/blog/2018/04/intersection-race-guns-schools-resources-teaching-times/.

Nijkamp, M. (2018). *This is where it ends.* Naperville, IL: Sourcebooks Fire.

Virginia Tech. (2018). *We remember.* Retrieved from https://www.weremember.vt.edu.

CHAPTER 11

Misdiagnosing Generational Trauma and Grief: I Am Not Angry; I Am Triggered and Grief Stricken

Nneka Greene

Well, I am tired. This tiredness comes from constant external destructive factors and generational trauma. My trauma manifests itself in ways that are confused with anger and irrationality. James Baldwin wrote, "It is certain, in any case, that ignorance allied with power, is the most ferocious enemy justice can have" (1972, p. 149). In the face of these injustices and trauma, grief is easier to swallow; it is easier to offer condolences when you believe that the pain is caused by some external force. Grief is an emotion that mirrors love, in that it is a part of our human existence. Grieving and its multifaceted processes are necessary to evaluate what has been lost and how grief will affect the survivor moving forward.

In the last few years, I have encountered grief that is not from the loss of a loved one. The experiences include assaults on my existence as a Black woman navigating a majority White academy, a Black woman living in a country that finds her skin dangerous, a Black woman working

N. Greene (✉)
Indiana Wesleyan University, Marion, IN, USA
e-mail: nneka.greene@agsfaculty.indwes.edu

© The Author(s) 2020   139
S. A. Shelton and N. Sieben (eds.),
Narratives of Hope and Grief in Higher Education,
https://doi.org/10.1007/978-3-030-42556-2_11

alongside law enforcement that continues to kill her unarmed kinsmen, a Black woman in conflict with a faith that supports the separation and denial of migrant families from safety and better lives. When discussing Frears and Schneider's (1981) wholistic framework model (*wholistic* is a term/spelling from their framework), there have been different phases identified in the grieving process, and this process encompasses different loss events with different levels of support given to those grieving. I created the following image and chart, based on Frears and Schneider (1981) to help me explore these concepts more fully:

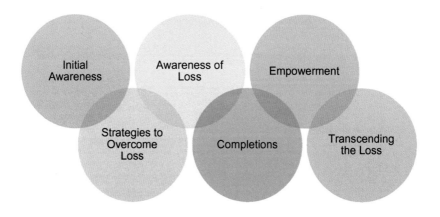

Phases	Description
Initial awareness	When loss first becomes a reality
Strategies to overcome loss	Holding on and letting go representing the adaptive defenses when loss is a threat
Awareness of loss	Extensive/intensive exploration of the loss
Completions	Phases of grief – healing, acceptance, and resolution
Empowering of self	Enhances the sense of personal power
Transcending the loss	Represents growth

Frears and Schneider's framework consists of phases of the grief process and what those phases may resemble while navigating the academy. These phases are not necessarily taken in order but are representative of common themes that the grieving endures. In short, the chart signifies the initial awareness of the incident that caused the grief or loss and ends with the individual transcending that loss and ultimately exhibiting growth.

INTELLECTUAL

Yes, education has been my saving grace. My academic journey started in urban-defined schools suffering from lack of resources and the stigma that its students were incapable of excellence. Baldwin (1961) expertly declared "anyone who has struggled with poverty knows how extremely expensive it is to be poor" (Para. 9). I was a high-achieving student but was never selected for any type of talented, high-achieving, or gifted education services. Dr. Donna Y. Ford, a prominent gifted education scholar, with a research specialty in desegregating gifted education, has found that students of color are often overrepresented in special education and underrepresented in gifted education (Ford, 1998). The denial of additional educational services in America's schools and the constant reinforcement of inferiority for students of color promote *stereotype threat* (Steele & Aronson, 1995) and impostor syndrome. Steele (2000) described stereotype threat as "[a] threat of being viewed through the lens of a negative stereotype or the fear of doing something that would inadvertently confirm that stereotype" (p. 679). As a student from an urban environment, I constantly fight internal struggles to prove my intellectual worth. I grieve daily for past generational traumas—when my ancestors were prohibited from learning how to read or write; from attending university; and from excelling without their intellect being questioned. Those traumas are constant reminders that I must do more—be more and accomplish more—than my White counterparts in order to achieve a similar semblance of worth. I work over holidays, when others are sleeping, during times of respite, because I must always be better. I remind myself that I am not an impostor, that I belong here. But I sure am tired.

The early works of Pauline Rose Clance and Suzanne Imes identified impostor syndrome as being more than simple insecurity (Roché, 2014). According to Peteet, Montgomery, and Weekes (2015), many matriculating Black students experience a sense of "intellectual phoniness known as the impostor phenomenon (IP)...often experienced by high achievers and underrepresented racial/ethnic minorities (URMs)" (pp. 175–176). Bernard, Hoggard, and Neblett's (2017) study posited that students experiencing IP often disregarded their accomplishments for internal abilities, while attributing those successes to external factors. My White peers compliment me on how well I am doing in my doctoral work, but I find it hard to accept compliments without doubt and trepidation. I know that I am worthy, but this trauma is ever-present—like a dark presence lurking in the shadows of my self-consciousness. Am I being complimented because my academic achievements are unexpected, or are they genuine? Let me tell you: I am tired. Tired of having to think about motives, tired of having to prove my worth.

ACTIVISM

The history of America's education system is undeniably one of privilege, discrimination, and inequity for those citizens who find ourselves on the other side of power and capital. Teachers, curricula, textbooks, and standardized tests have reinforced the inequity that is the foundation of America's educational institutions. As a public school student educated in the inner-city of Philadelphia, I had just enough educational assistance to pass the necessary standardized tests, but I was deprived of learning about the historical and rich contributions that my ancestors made to society. Baldwin (1963) declared "the paradox of education is precisely this—that as one begins to become conscious one begins to examine the society in which he is being educated" (Para. 2). My desire to attend a Historically Black College and University (HBCU) for my undergraduate education was fed by an absolute hunger for continuous reinforcement of racial pride and positive racial identity.

I remember being met with stares while visiting a Predominately White Institution (PWI) in Pennsylvania during my junior year of high school. I remember feeling like an exhibit in a museum. As we entered the dining hall, my fellow classmates and I were met with gaping mouths and uncomfortable stares. I left that tour vowing to not attend a PWI—to not even apply to a PWI, no matter how much in-state tuition I was offered. I felt less-than—not a feeling that a teenager should experience while considering postsecondary education. That experience solidified my decision to attend an HBCU. During that first year, I was a newly registered voter, and I participated in the political arena, being introduced to activism through a student-led sit-in on campus.

Developing students to be critical thinkers and world changers should include activism, especially with the changing political and social change in a democracy. America's continued inequities in education, including objections to affirmative action, continued lack of culturally sustaining pedagogies, and implicit/explicit biases produce recurring trauma experienced by students of color, no matter the education attainment level. Academic communities' expectations that higher education help to redress societal wrongs have increased campus activism (Altbach, 2016). Models of this activism from the recent past include the anti-war and civil rights movements of the 1960s, and anti-racism, -sexism, -xenophobia, and -homophobia movements of contemporary higher education. The scenes of sit-ins, segregated drinking fountains, snarling police dogs, and angry suburban segregationists are not concealed or forgotten in America's shameful past and, the residual effects of these injustices continue. Students of color are continuously forced to pay a Black tax (i.e., additional costs that people of African descent pay—academically—for their skin tone). My ancestors have been paying this tax for centuries, and it has been transferred generationally. I am tired, but the work does not end until the taxing system is dismantled and we achieve true liberation.

Spiritual Hope

It was 1999. I was a new college graduate and newly separated from the Army—a very brief stint because of injury. I had earned an undergraduate degree in criminal justice but was lost in a society that often saw my brown skin as criminal. I experienced spasms of grief when faced with my lack of professional opportunities. However, I found hope through spirituality. For decades, my Christianity had provided an outlet for my many questions about society's ills. I sought scripture for guidance in a world dimmed by injustice and despair. Johnson, Williams, and Pickard (2016) asserted that "religious/spiritual coping is dealing with stressful life events through beliefs and practices that are based around religion or are spiritual in nature" (p. 61), and this coping strategy is prevalent and promoted in the lives of religious African American women.

However, the election of former US President Barack Obama turned my Christian convictions upside down after. Many people used social media as a platform to simultaneously share racist opinions and dissent about the president and to espouse their Christian morals. How could these same people claiming to be Christians spew such hate and vitriol about a man and his family? How were evangelical Christians so easily offended that America had elected a president who looked different from the previous 43? The eloquent words of Baldwin maintained "please try to remember that what they believe, as well as what they do and cause you to endure does not testify to your inferiority but to their inhumanity" (Baldwin, 1962, Para. 7). Marsden (1997) acknowledged that conservative Christians have a poor record of accommodating people of color and women, and 2008's election was a reminder of that long-standing fact. This moment uprooted and disrupted my Christian ideologies and beliefs. I struggled and grieved, while trying to exist and survive with the intersectionality of my religious, gender, racial, and ethnic identities. These four identities have been under constant assault; cognitive dissonance is my constantly lived experience in a nation that is purposeful about perpetuating openly discriminatory practices.

Of course, these issues are not new. Christianity has a sordid past with African diaspora believers. Some argue that Christianity is the religion of the oppressors and has stripped believers of African descent of their ancestral beliefs and traditions. As an African American Christian, I am constantly at odds with what I believe and the actions of those who claim to share similar Christian virtues and values. The pervasiveness of Black Christian churches and White Christian churches is as American as apple pie and echoes back to memories of segregation in America. These separations create a contrasting reality that is a source of spiritual grief for me. And, Donald Trump being declared the current US President exacerbates that grief. Today, numerous evangelical Christians openly support him, a man who is constantly at odds with biblical tenets, such as compassion, honesty, trustworthiness, and love. My Sunday mornings are now a constant place of uncertainty and mourning.

US religious conservatives have become poster children for the current US presidency and administration. This politically right-leaning community and their approval of the current administration's behavior continue to memorialize the trauma of the marginalized, as they actively avoid denouncing oppressive policies and hateful rhetoric. Dismissing the needs and concerns of minoritized communities is continuing the promotion of White Patriarchy and Supremacy, and a large, powerful portion of Christian Evangelicals lead that charge. Williams (2016) opined, "seeing white as normal is part of the ideology of white supremacy" (p. 23), and "the power of white-as-normal is so common that it regulates social and political structures, often without participants recognizing that they are its willing disciples" (p. 25). Williams points out that the historical depictions of a White Jesus and God, which give "religious justification to the normative role of whiteness and those who are [Christians] are called to reveal and to arrest the enduring ideology of white supremacy" (p. 25). Being told Christian tenets such as, "love thy neighbor," "forgive, lest ye are not forgiven," and "turn the other cheek" are tiring. I am disgusted, particularly when I witness my Christian brothers and sisters as members of the Ku Klux Klan, hiding behind white sheets and blackface in college yearbooks, while being in pulpits and church pews on Sundays. As a mother of a teenager who enrolled at a predominately White Christian college in the Fall of 2019, I am concerned with the indoctrination that she will receive. I am nervous about the "love thy neighbor" mindset that I suspect she will be asked to uncritically adopt; after all, her neighbor may not feel the same about her. I am tired. Lord knows I am. I ask myself is loving thy neighbor still practical?

ATTITUDINAL

I am of dark complexion and have come to find my skin beautiful—reflective of God's light. That has not always been the case. I am the child of a dark-skinned mother and a fair-skinned, reddish-brown haired father. My very fair-skinned paternal grandmother told me that I could not possibly belong to my father because of my dark skin. My father held those same sentiments, left, and never returned. That is the beginning memory of an 8-month-old Black baby girl who was left to be raised by a proud single Black mother.

While attending elementary school and well into middle and high schools, adults claimed that I was "mouthy" because I always stood up for what I believed was right. Earning straight As did not shield me from teachers' verbal reprimands. I was known as the smart girl with the "smart mouth." Research overwhelmingly reflects my experiences and continues to do harm to Black children. Black children are punished more harshly than their White counterparts in school. Black boys are deemed scary and aggressive, while Black girls are deemed fast, loud, attitudinal, and angry (Lopez, 2018). These tropes do not end as Black children mature but unfortunately they follow them into adulthood, even in settings far-removed from schooling. Baldwin's words have never been more true, "I can conceive of no Negro native to this country who has not, by the age of puberty, been irreparably scarred by the conditions of his life" (Baldwin, 1984, p. 71). For example, Olympic gold medalist Serena Williams was recently penalized at a US Open for showing displeasure during a tennis match; which arguably cost her the match (Davis, 2018). Conversely, White women and men have behaved similarly or worse in the same sport and have never been met with such punishment and ridicule from commentators and sports pundits. As a Black professional I am conscious about how my passion might be misconstrued for anger and attitude. I have to code switch—which is the ability to alternate between two or more linguistic languages—daily, in order to appear more tolerable in my setting. This additional consciousness and required decision making is added emotional trauma.

Well into my doctoral studies, I found myself being apologetic for my pro-African American and anti-racism stances. As a Black doctoral student interested in social justice and equity in education, I sometimes find myself the lone advocate in my doctoral studies when discussing societal inequalities. My cohort peers likely have wondered about me, "Why is everything about race?" and "Why is she mad *now*?" I am the "Angry Black Woman." I have found Baldwin's words to ring true "the American idea of racial progress is measured by how fast I become white" (1979, Para. 14).

The Angry Black Woman (ABW) narrative is applied to any Black woman who purposefully disrupts and/or disavows whiteness, color-blind advocacy, bias, privilege, patriarchy, and White Supremacy. I encounter the same aggressive and assertive trope in the workplace whenever I stand up to White coworkers, who are purposefully harming my fellow Black colleagues. My actions are deemed overly assertive, while a male coworker would be applauded for his decisiveness and assertiveness. According to a study completed by Corbin, Smith, and Garcia (2018), the ABW storyline has a historical legacy in American race-gendered stereotypes perpetuated in and through mass media and culture. We are often seen as aggressive, loud, masculine, angry, and less worthy of protection than our White women counterparts.

To exist in a world where I am judged by my attributes and not my outward appearance would be remarkable, but this seems to be utterly impossible. In my travels outside of the USA, I similarly find myself instantly labeled "Black." There is no blending-in in countries where I am the minority—even sometimes a novelty. As I visited Athens, Greece, my dinner party found a quaint table, and as we prepared to indulge in dolmas and a shot of ouzo, a loud yell pierced the quiet evening: "AFRICA!!" As we looked up, there was a man we assumed to be Greek running and pointing at our table—the only table with patrons of color. While in Edinburgh, Scotland, a friend and I shopped in a little store packed with tourists and a plethora of tartan hanging from its windows. As we browsed for souvenirs, it became apparent that we were the only ones being followed, while other customers were left completely unattended. These instances have contributed to my perpetual state of grief as I navigate the world with my brown skin.

My children are often the lone students of color in class pictures. My educational research topics are usually the only ones centered on anti-racism, social justice, and culturally sustaining pedagogies. This is surprising, because all of my interactions are with School of Education doctoral students. I wonder, "What does the future look like for my children? Are these pre-service teachers and administrators in my doctoral courses interested in disrupting a system that is failing and suppressing marginalized students?" These thoughts make me tired: tired for the present, tired for future work, tired for my children, tired for my children's children.

My Black existence is the one constant in my life. Unfortunately, the daily traumas are omnipresent and require survival strategies that parallel those needed for dystopian societies. These experiences existed throughout my life, and in nearly any space I might occupy. I recently spoke to a White classmate of mine and shared this narrative:

> Imagine that for your entire life you were identified as being Black, and immediately judged accordingly. No matter where you go, what country you travel to, store you shop in, your skin speaks for you before you open your mouth. Imagine watching people like you being killed in the streets by law enforcement without penalty. Imagine your children not receiving the same education as their White classmates. Imagine having to prove your existence and right to belong in a space because of your skin. Imagine being fearful when seeing the lights from a police cruiser in your rear window. Imagine not knowing someone's true intentions when meeting them—are you just the quota for the I-have-Black friends mentality? Imagine waking up every morning not knowing how your home country will attempt to degrade, demean, or destroy you? Would that make you angry? Would that cause your grief? Would that tire you?

My classmate stood in awe. He shared how he couldn't imagine living like that every day. My only ask was whether he would consider these thoughts the next time that he assumed that a Black person was exhibiting anger. He agreed he would. I let him know I am tired: tired of having to explain.

STRATEGIES FOR HOPE

Intellectual Strategies

One major strategy I have implemented to find hope is seeking out same-race mentors in academia. My current institution fulfills portions of my spiritual needs; however, the need to be mentored by those who also suffer from and personally understand transgenerational and historical trauma is important for my survival and self-empowerment. In my search for academic family and support, Dr. Donna Y. Ford, one of the founders of R.A.C.E. (Research, Advocacy, Collaboration, Empowerment) Mentoring (or RM) Facebook group, located me in another group and welcomed me with open arms. RM was founded to assist Black and Hispanic scholars with navigating an overwhelmingly White academy. Black senior scholars share their experiences of journeying to and through academia's ivory tower. Several members of RM, including some of RM's original founders, have collaborated and published books sharing their lived experiences in higher education. One particularly helpful resource to me has been *R.A.C.E. Mentoring Through Social Media: Black and Hispanic Scholars Share Their Journey in the Academy.* The book's sections explore the lived experiences of Black and Hispanic scholars navigating the academy as doctoral students, assistant professors, associate and full professors, higher education administrators and P-12 educators and administrators. RM, its founders, and books such as this one work "to tackle the numerous thorny and contentious issues and challenges in higher education" (Ford, Trotman-Scott, Going, Wingfield, & Henfield, 2017, p. x).

Mental Health and Spiritual Strategies

I find myself tired and triggered daily with the constant bombardment of macro- and microaggressions in school, the workplace, and everyday living. How do I survive when I'm incessantly inundated with external trauma and internal suffering? How do I disallow anger to become all-consuming? In the African American community and its churches, mental health is not regularly discussed. As a Christian, I was always told to "pray and not worry," "to trust God," and that "God will never forsake you." None of these statements are actual remedies for the declining mental health of those suffering from generational trauma. It took me almost four decades to realize that my mental health was just as important as my physical, spiritual, and financial health. Mental health was never a topic of conversation growing up, nor was it discussed from the church pulpit. I have found meditation, journaling, and quiet times helpful in coping with the overwhelming amount of external trauma and grief. These strategies provide a pathway to hope.

Attitudinal Strategies

I have come to understand that my righteous indignation is a survival mechanism. Ashley (2014) opined that "hostility, rage, aggressiveness, and bitterness may be reflective of survival skills developed by Black women" (p. 28). The brain processes daily, overwhelming, and continuous oppression as anger in the amygdala, a region that is particularly responsive to social interaction (Ashley, 2014). I am hyper-aware of my triggering moments and am working with a therapist to master self-soothing techniques. I am also ceasing to apologize for my Blackness, dopeness, trauma, and for how I deal with it all in the face and the space of pervasive injustice and oppression.

Returning to Frears and Schneider's (1981) wholistic framework, the additional steps of grief (i.e., awareness of loss, completion, empowering of self, transcending the loss) are recognizable steps after identifying coping strategies. The awareness of loss is necessary before one might implement survival strategies for grieving. Often, it seems that more familiar and obvious forms of grief, such as losing a loved one, come with familiar forms of support, such as prayer, social support, and expressions of sympathy. However, when loss and grief are the result of oppressive social structures, loss is less evident, and modes of support are less familiar and less likely. The result can be prolonged, and even an internalized, grieving process (Frears & Schneider, 1981).

Grief is an inescapable human condition, but the nature of the grieving process depends on many internal (e.g., self-care, mental, physical, spiritual well-being) and external (e.g., support) factors, which are variably available to the grief-stricken. These modes of grief shape higher education, too, and students, faculty, and staff need grief support, whether a result of lost loved ones or sociopolitical traumas like racism, while navigating the academy. In considering my own perspectives, I have realized that many scholars arrive in higher education with generational trauma. Unfortunately, academia tends to dismiss grief as unworthy of institutional support. I shared a testimony with other doctoral students in the School of Education at my last doctoral residency:

> I am the little Brown girl from the housing projects of Philadelphia. I have seen a dead body and can identify the smell of crack cocaine. My mother was the smartest woman I have ever met with a high school education. She loved to read. So, I followed in her footsteps and took up reading as a way to escape. I excelled in school and realized *that* was my way to stand out from my community. My zip code identified me as "the little Brown girl from the ghetto," so my grades had to make up for it. I worked extremely hard but arrived at school with unseen traumas and grief. One of my closest friends was murdered over a weekend, but I had to attend school the next Monday. There were no grief counselors, so I internalized it and kept moving. My reminder to doctoral students is to remember that you could have a student like me in their class. They are not loud, scary, attitudinal, or angry.

I reminded my higher education cohort members that those same traumatized children grow up to be traumatized adults without proper help. It is important to be culturally sensitive to the varying communities that reside in a classroom. These differences include religions, socioeconomic status, immigration status, etc. Higher education's job is to educate the whole student; failure to do so upholds and prolongs the grieving process, and the oppressions that created those traumas in the first place. I am that student. I am also a higher education instructor. I am indeed tired. I am grief stricken. I am worn, but I AM NOT ANGRY. I am hopeful. I am a SURVIVOR.

References

Altbach, P. G. (2016). Harsh realities. In M. N. Bastedo, P. G. Altbach, & P. J. Gumport (Eds.), *American higher education in the twenty-first century* (4th ed., pp. 84–109). Baltimore, MD: Johns Hopkins University Press.

Ashley, W. (2014). The angry Black woman: The impact of pejorative stereotype on psychotherapy with Black women. *Social Work in Public Health, 29*(1), 27–34. https://doi.org/10.1080/19371918.2011.619449.

Baldwin, J. (1961). *Nobody knows my name.* New York, NY: Vintage Books.
Baldwin, J. (1962). *My dungeon shook: A letter to my nephew on the one hundredth anniversary of the emancipation.* Retrieved from https://progressive.org/m agazine/letter-nephew/.
Baldwin, J. (1963). A talk to teachers. *The Saturday Review.* Retrieved from http://richgibson.com/talktoteachers.htm?fbclid=IwAR3hLitIsZV2g5h 3W8D8mRfrIjfb35HEA860V75rpHIMJ2o6n42p3L2dQ6k.
Baldwin, J. (1972). *No name in the street.* New York, NY: Vintage Books.
Baldwin, J. (1979). On language, race and the black writer. *Los Angeles Times.* Retrieved from https://radicalscholarship.wordpress.com/2017/02/22/ every-white-person-in-this-country-knows-one-thing-james-baldwin-1979/.
Baldwin, J. (1984). *Notes of a native son.* Boston, MA: Beacon Press.
Bernard, D. L., Hoggard, L. S., & Neblett, E. W. (2017). Racial discrimination, racial identity, and impostor phenomenon: A profile approach. *Cultural Diversity & Ethnic Minority Psychology, 24*(1), 1–11. https://doi.org/10.1037/cdp 0000161.
Corbin, N. A., Smith, W. A., & Garcia, R. (2018). Trapped between justified anger and being the strong Black woman: Black college women coping with racial battle fatigue at historically and predominantly white institutions. *International Journal of Qualitative Studies in Education, 31*(7), 626–643. https://doi.org/10.1080/09518398.2018.1468045.
Davis, W. (2018). Serena Williams fined $17,000 for 3 code violations in U.S. Open final. *NPR.* Retrieved from https://www.npr.org/2018/09/08 /645919944/naomi-osaka-wins-u-s-open-in-upset-after-serena-williams-gets-game-penalty.
Ford, D. Y. (1998). The underrepresentation of minority students in gifted education: Problems and promises in recruitment and retention. *The Journal of Special Education, 32*(1), 4–14.
Ford, D. Y., Trotman-Scott, M., Going, R., Wingfield, T. T., & Henfield, M. S. (Eds.). (2017). *R.A.C.E. mentoring through social media: Black and Hispanic scholars share their journey in the academy.* Charlotte, NC: Information Age.
Frears, L. H., & Schneider, J. M. (1981). Exploring loss and grief within a wholistic frameworks. *Personal & Guidance Journal, 59*(6), 341–345.
Johnson, S. D., Williams, S. L., & Pickard, J. G. (2016). Trauma, religion, and social support among African American women. *Social Work & Christianity, 43*(1), 60–73.
Lopez, G. (2018). Black kids are way more likely to be punished in school than white kids, study finds. *Vox.* Retrieved from https://www.vox.com/identit ies/2018/4/5/17199810/school-discipline-race-racism-gao.
Marsden, G. M. (1997). *The outrageous idea of Christian scholarship.* New York, NY: Oxford University Press.

Peteet, B. J., Montgomery, L., & Weekes, J. C. (2015). Predictors of impostor phenomenon among talented ethnic minority undergraduate students. *Journal of Negro Education, 84*(2), 175–186.

Roché, J. (2014). Conquering impostor syndrome: Lessons from female and minority business leaders. *Leader to Leader, 2014*(74), 13–18. https://doi.org/10.1002/ltl.20147.

Steele, C. M. (2000). Stereotype threat and African American student achievement. In D. B. Grusky, C. K. Manwai, & S. Szelenyi (Eds.), *Social stratification: Class, race & gender in sociological perspective* (pp. 678–683). New York, NY: Perseus Books.

Steele, C. M., & Aronson, J. (1995). Stereotype threat and the intellectual test performance of African Americans. *Journal of Personality and Social Psychology, 69*(5), 797–811.

Williams, R. (2016). Seeing whiteness. *Christian Century, 133*(15), 22–25.

CHAPTER 12

En las sombras: A Letter to My Friend About Grief, Desire, and Haunting

Lucía I. Mock Muñoz de Luna

Nour, my dear friend,

I hope that my letter finds you well, and that you are finding time for yourself. I know from the news that the refugee camp in Lebanon, your home, is once again the site of protests—I hope you, your family, and friends are safe. You've been on my mind often since the last time that we saw each other, and I'm writing about some of the things that we talked about then (Tuck, 2019). Much of our time that week—three months now, seems so long ago—was spent sitting together as you mourned the sudden loss of your closest friend. My heart aches for you and her family now, as it did then; across the distance between us, I can still feel the sadness that was your constant companion as we walked the city streets, and you told me stories of a friendship that spanned a lifetime.

Nour, this letter is about grief and how it has entangled itself in both our lives, and in our friendship. Of course, it also about so much more, but grief seems like a good, if difficult, place to start. You often quote

L. I. Mock Muñoz de Luna (✉)
University of North Carolina at Chapel Hill, Chapel Hill, NC, USA
e-mail: lucia.mock@unc.edu

S. A. Shelton and N. Sieben (Eds.),
Narratives of Hope and Grief in Higher Education,
https://doi.org/10.1007/978-3-030-42556-2_12

153

Palestinian poet Mahmoud Darwish to explain things to me, so I use him here to help untangle why I feel the need to write to you about something so complicated. Darwish (2008) once said that Palestine is a grief-stricken land, and I will venture to say that the refugee camp where you live is an extension of your homeland: it, too, is a grief-stricken land. It is a place, who along with its people, has survived seventy years of wars, massacres, exclusion, and poverty. (Nour, I've used "who" for the camp on purpose. Drawing from Sara Ahmed's [2018] writing on use and "mis-use" to assert that the land is a non-human but *living* being—a *teacher*—it is more a "who" than a "what," I think.)

As I write this letter, you are in constant worry that the United Nations-run schools and hospitals that your community relies on for survival will shut down because the United States has ceased financial support. You are a land and a people who are being actively written out of existence by violence, in all its insidious, mundane forms (Sharif, 2016). I am a sometimes-visitor in this land, in your home, and I am trying to understand this grief, because I want to better understand *you*. Our lives are intertwined now: our work together in the school that you started in your community five years ago has bound us together. We are connected through our shared love of learning and our commitment to seeing through what education can do for the lives of young people and for the survival of a community, a people. The past five years have also seen our friendship grow into something neither of us expected—we've gone from strangers who only greeted one another with a hesitant handwave and hello, to then having coffee each Saturday morning in your office, to where we are now, which feels almost nameless. You once said to my mother that you would take care of me like I was one of your sisters; and though you probably said that only to comfort her, I take you at your word and will care for you in the same way. And because the ties that bind me to you and the camp are also what tethers me to my own sense-of-self, I want to spend some time feeling them, looking at them, tugging at them to see what comes loose.

In some ways, I see this refugee camp—your home—as a land of ghosts; a place that is haunted and haunting. These ghosts are more than apparitions or shadows of the formerly-living; they are the living, vibrant embodiments of your grief. What can I possibly mean by this? I'll tell you a story. Earlier today my mother and I spoke about her journey through education and learning. I had sent her an article written by Leigh Patel (2016), in which learning is posed as a fugitive act. In her writing, Patel draws a distinction between schooling as a form of social control, and learning as a fundamentally different venture that forces us away from what is known and toward an unknowable future—fugitive in the sense of a departure. I sent Dr. Patel's article to my mom because her journey, in many ways, reflects this distinction between schooling and learning. Like you, she was not able to stay in school as long as she wanted—but for different reasons. Both of you were kept from pursuing your education, and you both often talk about what you would have been able to accomplish had you continued. Access to education, or a lack thereof, shaped your worlds in many ways—and you both grieve this loss. But from that loss, you have both re-formed your lives through your desires to learn—and to transgress. You have forged a path to and through learning that is rooted in something more powerful than the structures that would suppress you.

Today my mom told me that she feels now that, through her daughters, she has been able to do what she could not as a young woman; that through us and our educational journeys, she has been able to explore new worlds and understandings. I often send her what I'm reading and writing, and she shares with me her thoughts—from her I have learned how to read the world, and now together we read the texts that build the academy around me in my doctoral studies. Learning has become fugitive, uncontainable. Today we also talked about the web of women that we have created through learning together—an intergenerational, transnational, transcultural web—that you now help us form. This space of intimacies is held together by threads of grief, along with a curiosity and desire to know and to live—to *be* in this world that would erase us if it could. If we let it. But we refuse this erasure with every breath, with every feeling, with every desire. These are the ghosts I'm speaking of: "I don't want to haunt you, but I will" (Morrison, 1987; Tuck & Ree, 2013, p. 644).

For the past year, I have been reading and thinking about desire, primarily through the writing of Eve Tuck, an Indigenous scholar who uses this concept to re-imagine the ways in which research and relationships might be envisioned and enacted. Much has been written about desire, but that's mostly by White men, and frankly, I would rather not have them tell me what desire is. Tuck's theory building around desire is the guiding voice in how I am coming to understand this concept. I will do my best to explain: for me, desire is tied to the physical but it also extends beyond that (Tuck, 2009). Desire is a way of knowing and understanding the world. In this case, it also encompasses and accompanies grief. Desire is "smart," "wise," "agentic," it is productive (Tuck, 2010, p. 636). It is part of who we are, and also guides what we want to know—an informed seeking (Tuck, 2009). Desire is what keeps you up at night, lights your body on fire, what you whisper to yourself—or maybe even to another— *en las de sombras de la noche*, as if the words contain some life and power beyond our control. It is the not yet and not anymore (Tuck, 2009). Tuck writes, alongside C. Ree, that: "Desire is what we know about ourselves, and damage is what is attributed to us by those who wish to contain us" (2013, p. 648). Often times, efforts to understand instead turn into a containment of self, or others. This narrowing, particularly in research, requires damage—narratives that document only brokenness and pain. While these have their purpose, they leave so much untold. Desire is what lurks in the shadow of these damage-centered narratives; it is a haunting.

> It accounts for the loss and despair, but also the hope, the visions, the wisdom of lived lives and communities. Desire is involved with the not yet and, at times, the not anymore. In many desire-based texts…there is a ghostly, remnant quality to desire, its existence not contained to the body but still derived of the body. Desire is about longing, about a present that is enriched by both the past and the future. It is integral to our humanness. (Tuck, 2009, p. 417)

There is so much here. Reading this—feeling these words out—helps me to connect the threads of grief, haunting, and desire. All are dangerous, all can be unpredictable—they are hard to pin down. Desire and grief are derived from the body but extend beyond it, beyond spatial and temporal borders. Tuck writes that "desire is an unstable element—it works by breaking down. Desire is radioactive" (2010, p. 641), which feels especially true to me—desire is unstable, unpredictable, and revolutionary. It refuses to be categorized, contained. Desire is radioactive and perhaps easier to dismiss than to attend to. But desire unattended is poison. This has been true in my own life, and I suspect it might hold true in yours as well. Grief might be what comes of desire deferred. Herein lies another haunting.

When I talk about haunting, I am talking about ghosts, but not in the sense of the ghoulish movie figure that terrorizes the protagonist until vanquished. The ghosts I describe are not ones we can get rid of. I've never liked horror movies—perhaps because of their incomplete rendering of what these specters are and how they come to be; or maybe because they just scare me. But haunting in the way I'm trying to describe to you now is, yes, scary, but not in the way that movies scare us for temporary thrills; rather, it is terrifying because it embodies and enacts all that we turn away from when we can. It is what—who—we ignore, in order to be able to continue living like we do. Haunting is a way of being, a refusal to be vanished, a lingering—and finally, it is an imprint, maybe even a documentation, of desire.

But why am I writing this to you, and why now? Since I last saw you, grief has been a constant presence in my mind, and a question haunts me: how can I—in everything I am and represent—accompany you, and your community, in your grief? Of course, there's so much more to this question, and maybe it does not make sense. Let me say it more plainly: I am Spanish, I am an American, I am an academic, I am a settler, and I am an *ajnabeeyeh* (*foreigner*, in Arabic); I am also more than this, but much of who I am is tied to the structures and forces that cause you pain and grief—so, can I be these things and also be a *compañera* to you in your grieving?

I am not necessarily looking for an answer from you at this moment—this is more of a question I have been asking myself these past few months. In many ways, I know that you have already let me be a part of your life. I can see you shaking your head at me with a teasing smile, and telling me that we need to get back to the work of figuring out how we are going to raise enough money to keep the school open this year. I promise that is what I will be working on tomorrow morning. But in the meantime, if you do have a response, I hope you will share it with me. What am I saying? Of course you will have an answer, and you have never been shy to tell me what is in your heart. And ultimately, the questions that I have posed in this letter can only really be answered by you and your community; my role in this extends only so far as you allow. There is use, though, in my consideration of these questions, in my reflection on how I can prepare myself to be an ethical receiver (Nagar, 2017) of your trust, of your stories—someone who, with unrelenting care and love, may hold and be worthy of the truths and desires you share.

I know that I write this letter selfishly, so please forgive me. A trusted colleague said to me earlier today that letter-writing is also an act of love, and I think that that is a true and beautiful sentiment. That also makes this harder to write, because my ways of being and knowing love are not ones you approve of. Although at times I suspect your mind is shifting somewhat (after you took a picture of a pride flag that said "love is love," you said you agreed with that idea, but you still see being gay as something wrong—you erased the picture so no one at home would know you took it); so my act of love here, and in everything I do at the camp, is haunted by what I don't tell you, for fear that you might turn your back on me. Call it deception, call it self-preservation; I write this letter but probably will never send it to you, and that is a ghost that walks with me in the camp, and always.

I have written this letter before but have never finished it. I also struggle to write about something that is not mine; something that I do not, and perhaps will never, understand. I felt—and feel—that what we do as visitors and researchers is take your people's pain and make it into something that we can parade around as ours, some proof of our expertise and caring, and as a way to somehow perversely prove your humanity to others. bell hooks writes:

> No need to hear your voice...Only tell me about your pain. I want to know your story. And then I will tell it back to you in a new way. Tell it back to you in a way that it has become mine, my own. Re-writing you, I write myself anew. (1989, p. 208)

My fear is that this re-writing is what I am doing with my work with you, and I would not forgive myself if that was the case. I've been witness to this too many times: two summers ago, on my first day back at the refugee camp where you live and where we work together, when you greeted me by making me immediately start answering your emails for you—the ones in English that take you too long to write—there was a foreign woman who came to the camp to interview women who had married at young ages. She was a friend of your colleague, so you allowed her to use one of the offices in the Women's Center to interview a girl who had married as a teenager and divorced shortly thereafter. After a few minutes, the foreign woman returned, frustrated that the girl would not talk to her. You followed the woman back into the office where the girl now sat alone, and when you came back a few minutes later, I could sense your irritation. I asked you about it, and you said something like: "Of course the girl didn't want to talk. Sometimes you foreigners don't know what questions to ask, or even how to ask them. But you always expect us to answer." You were right. We often only ask questions that will provide us with answers that we want, answers limited by our understandings of our—and your—existence. Yet, we ask the questions anyway, and demand answers. A few weeks later you and I were sitting on the floor of your office organizing receipts when we started talking about why people come to visit the camp in the first place. You asked me if it was to see your sad and poor lives. To see a different kind of poverty. To be able to say that we had visited a Palestinian refugee camp. The answer to all of this is: yes, there is a fetish for pain both in academia and the world of non-profits; a need to prove your humanity and justify our sympathy and support (Tuck & Yang, 2014) by witnessing and then retelling your pain. But you already know this. You've told me often that you are not just pictures for us to hang up on our walls.

The response I hear from those around me—my colleagues and mentors in this institution of higher learning—is:

> But what are we to write about, if not their sad and poor lives, their loss, their grief? How can we help them otherwise? Who populates a grief-stricken land if not for those stricken, and the ghosts who haunt them?

Forgive my bluntness, but to me, these questions are a distraction; they lack imagination, and they are boring (Tuck, 2018). They search for nothing beyond the pictures that hang up on our walls. They deny a fuller picture of humanity. My aversion to these questions is by no means an attempt to deny your pain, or to silence your telling of those stories. These are your stories to tell, when and as you see fit. Instead, it is an attempt to affirm that you are not just pictures or pain stories, and to reckon with the fact that you are right: we researchers often don't know what questions to ask. What would happen if we tried to ask different questions of you, and of ourselves? What does grief really mean to us anyway? Who decides what grief is, and who gets to feel it? How do we even begin to grieve a loss that is interminable (Sharpe, 2016)?

Since I started my doctoral studies I've had the creeping doubt that feeling grief, particularly in the Eurocentric culture I've grown up in, has been made a limited, linear process that requires categorization (Patel, 2018). It's a process that, if it lasts too long or is too deeply felt, is pathology. There are stages to grief, and we progress through them, until we come to acceptance. And the sadness has been relegated to some sort of manageable past. Perhaps my conceptions of sadness are too tied to this linearity, this drive to standardize emotion. I am frustrated and angry at this thought, because not only are we responsible for so much of what has caused your pain, but we also name it and then set its limitations. We cause your sadness and then tell you how to experience it. I am complicit in this, and it makes me wonder what I have missed in my need to translate what you've told me into this process, and into words like trauma or self-regulation (Goldhill, 2019). Like Eve Tuck and C. Ree (2013) write, you were telling me a story, but maybe I was hearing a different one. One of the greatest gifts you've given me is to keep telling me the story until I've started to hear it the way you want me to. And of course, these stories acknowledge the very real and deep pain of loss. There is certainly a need to name the crimes in order to refute them (Tuck & Yang, 2014). The issue is with only seeing your story as one of loss and the ensuing grief; that somehow hope and grief—and desire—exist on some sort of linear path, far away from one other and kept separate by these myopic understandings. One thing that I am certain of is that there is use in trying to transgress the boundaries of being and knowing that have been placed between us and our understandings of these feelings. It is worth taking the time to answer these questions together, and to come to conclusions—and beginnings—that are more complicated, more human, more incomplete than the ones that we think that we have now.

But grief is a good place to start, because it is something we are familiar with, and it allows me to write to you about desire, which I'm realizing is what this letter is really about. I believe that desire and grief are intimately tied together, both springing from that miraculous human ability to love as deeply as we do. bell hooks (1989) posits that we are all connected through emotion—that across all differences, we are bound together in our emotional universe, the shared realm of feeling. I believe that this is true, and that you and I have built our friendship on that understanding. This is why, despite my misgivings and doubts about my ability to fully comprehend your world, I am writing you this letter. This grief-stricken land that contains and nourishes our friendship is also a land that is, like us, full of desire, and it is along these desire paths (Ahmed, 2017) that you and I can walk together, our meandering footsteps forming a new route through this complicated place.

Since I first stepped into the camp, grief has been a constant presence and companion—ghosts lurking in the corner of each home, a feeling that follows people around like a shadow. Sometimes it has followed me: when we walk through the cramped alleyways of the camp, with the buildings so close that they block out the sun, with electrical wires hanging so precariously that you have to duck your head to avoid them, with water from burst pipes flowing like a creek downhill—almost as if showing us the way to your house. We pass by doors that are open, and sometimes inside these doors sits a woman looking out into the street, or into her kitchen, sitting silently as the TV hums or as children around her play. In the second that it takes to walk by and catch a glimpse of her or meet her searching eyes, to see how a few rays of sun have made it through the spaces between the buildings to illuminate her face, she seems like an apparition: a life and a story and a multitude of beings that haunt. *Tan bonita que amenaza* (Vila Tobella, 2018). And maybe I am the same to her. But her face haunts me, as do all the stories she might have told me had I just stopped to listen.

The shadows in the camp whisper to me stories of loss. Loss of rights, loss of agency, loss of land that was your home and companion, the loss of futures—and most of all, the loss of those you love(d). These losses, and the grief that accompanies them, as I have witnessed, are for you ever-present, non-linear, complicated, and often overwhelming; a feeling that envelops this community of people whose losses feel immeasurable.

But these losses are not all the result of unavoidable tragedy. Replace "loss" with "theft" in the paragraph above, and it might be more accurate. Your losses are marked by injustices; not all are inevitable losses, and many are marked by intentional, brutal violence. When using more active words like "theft" and "erasure," I see how grief becomes more clearly tied to justice. Tuck and Yang have written that justice is somewhere between grievance and grief (2016); redress for these thefts and losses is impossible, yet the desire for remedy and reparation persists (Tuck & Yang, 2014), and the ability to imagine futures outside of this moment depends on grief and the desire that accompanies it. Ashon Crawley asked, "What are the intimacies held in the space in which ghosts appear?" (Crawley, 2018). In the earlier questions that I posed about what we might write about besides your grief, I was trying to emphasize that sometimes your grief is all that we, as outsiders, are able—or want—to see. However, a narrative of *only* grief, of *only* damage, helps us to stay in an always-unfinished project of fixing what is broken—that which we have broken and are breaking. What is possible beyond this project? What intimacies exist in this space? What justice?

I see grief, haunting, and desire woven together, a pattern emerging in our shared story. What intimacies exist here? Perhaps these desire-ful ghosts that I've written to you about are haunting all of us. Perhaps they do so in different ways—for you, as the *not yet* and *not anymore*: the loss and despair, but also the longing and visions, the hopes for an inconceivable future (Tuck & Yang, 2018). The grief and desires these ghosts—and you—carry are powerful. You are haunted, but you are also haunting. For those of us who would try to erase you, these hauntings might be the "relentless remembering and reminding that will not be appeased by settler society's assurances of innocence and reconciliation" (Tuck & Ree, 2013, p. 642). In every desire, you refuse to be written out of existence; your grief serves as a reminder of crimes we try to forget. Your haunting is an act of defiance, of survivance (Vizenor, 2008). As your *compañera*—one with whom you break bread—how can I accompany you in your desires and hauntings? Can I carry in my body some of the whispers of revenge, *rechazo*, and survival that populate your grief-stricken and desire-ful land? These whispers are the settler's nightmare—both the reckoning that, despite our best efforts, these ghosts will continue to haunt, and that the reconciliation that we seek for our endless wrongs will not come—at least not in the current configuration of the world (Tuck & Ree, 2013). These hauntings are ever-present, non-linear, complicated, and often overwhelming, a feeling that envelops this community of people whose desires feel immeasurable.

But I think I'm beginning to do away with the notion of having to measure everything. I'm also less inclined to think that this letter needs an ending, or some sort of resolution. So, rather than end this letter on a hopeful note, I'll follow your example and end with a note of persistence. I've asked myself how I can be your *compañera* despite how complicated this all is, but maybe the question itself is enough—for now. The act of love implied in the word *compañera* promises persistence, a commitment, an act of nourishment marked by reciprocity; it demands a radical vulnerability and humility (Nagar, 2017). This is something that I will continue working toward. Perhaps that's the most we can offer each other through the grief and desires that mark our lives, our lands.

My friend, I hope to see you soon, *insha'Allah*. Until then, *estoy contigo*.

Lucía.

REFERENCES

Ahmed, S. (2017). *Living a feminist life*. Durham, NC: Duke University Press.
Ahmed, S. (2018). *Queer use*. Retrieved from https://feministkilljoys.com/2018/11/08/queer-use/.

Crawley, A. (2018). Ghosts. *The New Inquiry*. Retrieved from https://thenewinquiry.com/ghosts/.

Darwish, M. (2008). *On his deathbed: A letter by Mahmoud Darwish*. Retrieved from https://www.alaraby.co.uk/english/blog/2017/8/10/on-his-deathbed-a-letter-by-mahmoud-darwish.

Goldhill, O. (2019). Palestine's head of mental health services says PTSD is a western concept. *Quartz*. Retrieved from https://qz.com/1521806/palestines-head-of-mental-health-services-says-ptsd-is-a-western-concept/.

hooks, b. (1989). *Yearnings: Race, gender and cultural politics*. Boston, MA: Southend Press.

Morrison, T. (1987). *Beloved* . New York, NY: Random House.

Nagar, R. (2017). Hungry translations: The world through radical vulnerability. *Antipode*, 1–22.

Patel, L. (2016). Pedagogies of resistance and survivance: Learning as marronage. *Equity & Excellence in Education, 49*(4), 397–401.

Patel, L. (2018). Justice as a lackey. In E. Tuck & K. W. Yang (Eds.), *Toward what justice? Describing diverse dreams of justice in education* (pp. 101–112). New York, NY: Routledge.

Sharif, L. (2016). Vanishing Palestine. *Critical Ethnic Studies, 2*(1), 17–39.

Sharpe, C. (2016). *In the wake: On Blackness and being*. Durham, NC: Duke University Press.

Tuck, E. (2009). Suspending damage: A letter to communities. *Harvard Educational Review, 79*(3), 409–427.

Tuck, E. (2010). Breaking up with Deleuze: Desire and valuing the irreconcilable. *International Journal of Qualitative Studies in Education, 23*(5), 635–650.

Tuck, E. (2018). *This is taking too long: Waiting on settler drives to mutual destruction*. Symposium presentation at the American Educational Research Association Conference.

Tuck, E. (2019). Introduction. In L. T. Smith, E. Tuck, & K. W. Yang (Eds.), *Indigenous and decolonizing studies in education: Mapping the long view* (pp. 1–23). New York, NY: Routledge.

Tuck, E., & Ree, C. (2013). A glossary of haunting. In S. Holman Jones, T. E. Adams, & C. Ellis (Eds.), *Handbook of autoethnography* (pp. 639–658). Walnut Creek, CA: Left Coast Press.

Tuck, E., & Yang, K. W. (2014). R-words: Refusing research. In D. Paris & M. T. Winn (Eds.), *Humanizing research: Decolonizing qualitative inquiry with youth and communities* (pp. 223–248). Thousand Oaks, CA: Sage.

Tuck, E., & Yang, K. W. (2016). What justice wants. *Critical Ethnic Studies, 2*(2), 1–15.

Tuck, E., & Yang, K. W. (2018). Introduction. In E. Tuck & K. W. Yang (Eds.), *Toward what justice? Describing diverse dreams of justice in education* (pp. 29–45). New York, NY: Routledge.

Vila Tobella, R. (2018). Pienso en tu mirá. On *El Mal Querer* [CD]. Spain: Sony Music.

Vizenor, G. (2008). *Survivance: Narratives of native presence.* Lincoln: University of Nebraska Press.

PART IV

Finding Hope Through Grief
and Its Questions

CHAPTER 13

"Yup, Just Him": Misconceptions and Our Table for Three

Jeff Spanke

2018

But here's the thing with holidays. They always have a way of unwrapping the various truths we've spent the year hiding under the donate-to-Goodwill piles in our closet, or in the darkest corners of our minds, or behind the den couch that somehow remains off-limits. They show us where we've been. Who we are, how we do, what we know, and why we keep going. They're sacred, in that regard. Precious and ugly and itchy and pure. And they're never what we remember.

We spent our holidays opening letters from elderly relatives with "Mr." crossed out and "Dr." written in concession. Packages containing sweaters, because when pressed sometime around Thanksgiving, I told my mom that I could use more sweaters. Our front door opened to guests with kids and slow cookers wrapped in towels; our hearts opened, of course, to the season; and our wallets opened for one more reason to make our son smile for fifteen minutes, all while the coffee brewed and

J. Spanke (✉)
Ball State University, Muncie, IN, USA
e-mail: jtspanke@bsu.edu

S. A. Shelton and N. Sieben (eds.),
Narratives of Hope and Grief in Higher Education,
https://doi.org/10.1007/978-3-030-42556-2_13

167

he perused the handwriting on the note from Santa thanking him for the half-eaten cookies. "You're right, Buddy; that writing does kind of look like mine…"

We spent the holidays watching our five nephews—all sweet, pre-K cherubs—tear through the cornucopias of ornament-adorned paper, heaping the crumpled debris in mounds around the tree, while my mother-in-law tiptoed through the melee, garbage bag in hand, gathering the tattered remains of days spent taping.

We broke bread with our closest friends, and watched as our son, once again, obliged our silent request to play with the other kids while the grown-ups had their grown-up time. He spent the season doing just that. Playing with little cousins, chasing the younger children of his parents' college friends, and relishing the power that comes from being the oldest *and* only.

And we have never been prouder. He doesn't ask for siblings anymore. He's stopped wondering why he doesn't have a brother or a sister, or why poker needs four players. He's mastered being bashful when passive-aggressive bus-stop moms ask him intrusive questions, and he'll never know or bestow hand-me-downs. As 2018 wound to a close, we knew that we had a good life. A fine kid in our second-grade, bespectacled, somewhat toothless son. The house and the jobs and our health and the rest. We knew that we were lucky and loved our living.

But we also knew the fragility of it all. The temporality of having arrived. That, at any moment, it could all be taken away. The house, the jobs, life. Because we've known loss. We've felt pain, suffered in privileged silence, and, still, we grieve. This is our life, and this is our truth, unwrapped, every December, for the world to see. Our table for three. Debris, cast among the vibrant wreckage of red wagons, toy tractors, and miniature velociraptors: torn concealment that never makes it to the garbage bag. Our truth is there, nestled under every dead pine, burnt bulb, flickering star, or droopy garland. And in its scars, it scares me. I know what I have in these scenes, these tapestries of shared memories that tether us as family. And my heart bursts with a love that I never knew possible before that first plastic stick bore its blue cross all those years ago. The one sprinkled with pee from the Massachusetts bathroom that showed us our future, like those magic eight-balls from our past.

But I still wish the holidays didn't take me back there. That dark space that never makes it on Facebook or Christmas cards. My heart's still beating, as our story keeps repeating.

2012

We waited for the heartbeat. That faint but discrete muffled sound of a helicopter pulsating from the womb. I looked to the screen for movement. Arms twitching, repositioning, kicking. Something. We'd seen it before, of course: heard the chopper and watched the doctor circle the patch of pixels between the legs. "A boy, no doubt," she smiled nearly two years and nine lifetimes ago. *That* room was bright, with inspiring posters of fountains and countless pictures of cute, toothless grins and green-crayon drawings of crappy wax castles tacked to the wall. Now, all was silence and latex and beeps and breaths and nothing.

It was the same room as last time.

The tech kept waving her wand across the belly, languishing with each stroke to muster some magic onto the black and white monitor flickering in the corner, taunting us with empty promises of a life without DNCs, IUDs, and "Nope, he's our only one." "The gel may be a little cold," they always warn you. Last time, my wife didn't notice. Today, we're both shivering. It was almost Christmas, after all. Good thing that we hadn't told anyone about the pregnancy yet. That would have made the holidays a real bummer.

As my wife scooped the lukewarm goo off her empty stomach and tugged her shirt back down like a sheet across a coffin, I stared at those drawings on the wall, those green wax castles, with their thank-you notes and signatures scribbled sloppily in the moats. The thatch-roofed villages and sprawling, snow-capped mountains blanketing the horizon. It was all so cheery and putrid and kiddy and shitty. Nothing about them was to-scale, and their perspectives just seemed off. The dragon hovering above the tower was three times bigger than the drawbridge; the Queen wore a crown that would've probably knocked her to death in the...hedges?...below. They really were stupid drawings.

At least the framed pictures of the fountains *looked* nice. But the corporatized Zen-nonsense plastered in bold block letters beneath images of rising mist and sunbeams and bliss did nothing to detract from the fact that their aesthetic counterparts—those faded, slightly-stained pages torn from the bindings of 85 cent, off-brand coloring books—were all made by kids who survived the goo and the wand and the beeping and the cold. And in a few days, their Santa Claus would come to town.

I forced a grin when the doctor said we could "try again," as if making life was as simple as riding a bike or hitting a baseball. "Just takes one, Jeff. Wait for your pitch!"

Since we both still had some time on our lunch breaks—we didn't need to schedule another appointment or anything—my wife and I decided that TGI Fridays would be a nice place to commiserate over plates of moderately priced, casual American dining. Though the nauseating displays of holiday cheer and over-zealous, under-rehearsed feigned niceties of our trainee server—Hi! Amber!—did nothing to help the pub kitsch and fried cheese-food go down any smoother. My drink was warm, the fries were cold, the floor was sticky, God hates us, and the bathroom reeked of last night's hubris. And it wasn't even Friday!

Nope, we still had three more days to figure out how to salvage our year. Three more days to decide how to lie to our bosses about why we've been a little quiet lately. Three more days to fight about what to get our blessing of a healthy baby boy for Christmas, praise Jesus; whether or not we should tell our families about the baby we just lost but never saw; what to say when they ask, yet again, why, after three successful, award-winning years teaching high school, I suddenly decided to resign; how to reconcile with myself that I actually got fired; how to justify lying about it; when I'll ever come to terms with what happened in March...; how to explain graduate school and academia and professor life and prelims and dissertating and summers off to people who think PhD stands for "piled high and deep," and that those, like me, who can't do, teach; and what the hell we were gonna do to make sure life found a way to get better, come January. Turns out the Mayans were kinda right.

2012 really sucked.

2010

She fell asleep during the second movie. After spending all day flying from Indianapolis to Boston, driving to Cape Cod, gorging ourselves on fresh seafood, craft brews, and other delectable, New England treats, *and* endeavoring to make it through a double-feature at what must have been the last drive-in theater left in the country, my wife had just about had it. So when she fell asleep on my shoulder while I finished watching Jackie Chan teach Will Smith's kid karate, I didn't think anything of it. We were both exhausted, for sure; it had been a long day. It all made sense, though, the next morning when, after coming out of the bathroom at our seaside

B&B, she quietly whispered into my pillow-covered ear that she had some news.

News. As if having a baby was the same as a BP oil spill or Chilean miners or LeBron taking his talents to South Beach. This wasn't *news*. This was both inconsequential to the rest of the world *and* the single greatest change our world had ever known. This wasn't some headline or Christmas card caption or Facebook update; this was our life's evolution, forever and ever, Amen.

And what lives we already had! My wife was well into her first-year as a promising development assistant for a major research university; I had just wrapped-up my first year as a high school English teacher in the rural American Midwest farmlands; we were chipping away at the mortgage for our idyllic little white ranch house; and now, it seemed, our time as a dual-income-no-kid couple was drawing to a close.

We spent the rest of our Boston trip enamored by the unknown. We playfully debated names while waiting for whales to spray us. We discussed schools while hiking the Freedom Trail. We held hands like kids through Cambridge and kept count of all the different kinds of strollers we could buy. We knew that we didn't want to tell anyone about the baby until the second trimester—things happen, we knew—but before we left, we did write a note in the *Memories* book in our B&B. Buried among the countless weathered pages of obscure nostalgia and anonymous secrecies, my wife and I thanked our hosts for their warmth, their delicious food, and for having the bathroom where a pee-covered piece of plastic revealed our future. It was a good trip. And a good summer. And a good fall.

That Christmas we opened baby clothes.

2016

Enclosed: A Letter, Deleted.

Greetings! Merry Merry, Family and Friends! Well, what a year it's been! Let's see, now where should we begin...We sold our first house in early May ☹ Cinco de Mayo, we should say ☺ Bueno! It was a great house with so many memories! It's where our baby was born, where Jeff taught high school *and* earned his doctorate (so proud, *Dr.* Spanke!!), and where Kate worked her way up the university ladder. Great times, great friends, great memories!!! We loved our seven years there...

After a brief stay with Jeff's parents (two weeks!!!), we moved into our new house and got ready to start our new life! Jeff landed a great tenure-track job as an Assistant Professor of English (chirp chirp!!), Kate started work as a Director of Development for a non-profit therapeutic horse-riding center (giddy-up!!), and our sweet baby boy started Kindergarten!! They really do grow up so fast ☺☺ Our new house didn't have any air-conditioning for three weeks after we moved in (yikes!!), but we survived the summer and have had a great fall with no end in sight! We also celebrated our ten-year anniversary (AHHH!!!) and are so grateful for a such a wonderful marriage, and are so looking forward to the next decade to come. Bring it on! ☺ ☺ We love our new house, our new neighbors, and our new life, so close to family, and so many fun things to do!!

We're really so grateful for everything we have! Especially all the new people in our lives who just love asking if we only have one kid. Or when we're going to have another one. Or why, as Christians (duh!) we wouldn't want more. ☺ Thank you, New Neighbors, for bringing up those memories again. ☺ ☺ ☺ You really just make us all feel so welcome by getting to know us better!! We've gotten so bored in our old house with not having to answer to anybody, it's been nice gouging old wounds.

You all have such beautiful children, you really do—and so many of them!!!—and we're so lucky to be able to watch them all grow-up as best-little-girl-snobby-whiny-bitchy-pretty-little friends and run through our yard and stare at our Only and be brats at the bus-stop and disobey you and cuss and run amok and make our son feel, um, *unique?* ☺☺ And we *really* love all your ideas about getting pregnant, and the advice you read online and all your stories and sympathies and judgy quips about how Some People Can Just Handle One ☺.

So true, *right!?!* Thank you all, just so much, for all of your business and for thinking ours is yours, too. Thank you for making the word "Just" hurt so much—like, every fucking time—and for making our son wonder how and why and when he's going to stop being Not Like The Other Kids.

Ugh, kids!! ☺

Thank you for letting yourselves in; seriously, don't ever bother knocking. ☺ Make yourselves comfortable! What's ours is yours, just take what you need!! Or want! Or, ya know, whatever! Besties forever, am I right?!?! And thanks, above all, for making us feel like we have something to offer the neighborhood, even if it's just barbecue pity.

Merry Christmas,

The Spankes, Jeff, Kate, and Yup, Just Him

2015

We put two pictures on the Christmas card. One of the three of us at the zoo: him on her back, me, backpack strapped on and tapped from a day of gabbing with in-laws. All of us sweaty and glowing and showing our love. One of the year's best, for sure.

The other picture is more formal. Performative, staged. Me, dressed in my doctoral robe, tassel and cap and all the trimmings. My wife and son in their Sunday bests, nestled at my side by the fountain on campus. It was a gorgeous day, roughly 72 h before graduation. We made a point of having our friends take the pictures in advance. We didn't want to mess with the crowds after the real ceremony. And they all turned out great. Definitely worthy of our fifty some-odd closest family and friends.

But of all of the pictures of me in my robe that mean something, my favorite is the one that my wife took during the hooding. From the front row of the first balcony, three stories above and hundreds of feet away from the stage. The image is blurry, the faces grainy and faded. The hood itself had knocked off my cap but still, leaning over the edge, my wife captured my eyes. My smile and my pride all beaming up at her. Of course, I had no way of knowing at the time, but as the speaker read my name and Dr. Jeffrey Spanke flashed on the screen behind me—and as I looked up into the darkened abyss of the packed rafters hoping to catch a glimpse of my family—our eyes met as the shutter snapped shut.

This was the last of my commencement ceremonies. The closing of years spent bemoaning in acrimony and loneliness why I lost my job and my kids and our kids and my purpose and ours. The end of cursing Santa for not bringing me the toy I wanted, and the end of seeking the worst in people so that I could sleep at night. The last three years had been the most excruciating and invigorating of my life, but my wife and I had finally forged a strength in our fragility. Our Christmas card showed a family intact, backpacks in tow, and no signs of fracture. But that picture she took from her seat, that was pure Us. Knocked off cap and blurry. Hurried and just a little off-center. No real focus, both of us healing, concealing our cries through our smiles and our eyes dead-locked from afar, albeit just briefly.

2013

Every Christmas my wife takes the pictures of us from throughout the year and makes personalized calendars for our moms as gifts. She does her best to match the pictures to the correct months, but sometimes she needs to cheat a little. April, for instance, is usually pretty boring; not much happens in September outside of maybe a football game, and sometimes all those summer pool parties just sort of blend together. The staples remain, of course. Birthdays, anniversaries, holidays. For the last two years, most of the months have showcased our son, and occasionally seasons go by without any appearance from either my wife or me. Still, these calendars always seem to be the high watermark of the holiday season; our moms praise my wife for her craftsmanship and skill as a photographer, and I playfully pout that no one thanked me for picking up the calendars from Wal-Green's earlier that morning.

Here's what didn't make the cut this year:

- January

    - Us, wondering if we should tell anyone about what happened in December.
    - Us, deciding not to.

- February

    - Us, telling everyone we're pregnant. Or *she's* pregnant?

- March

    - Us, telling everyone she miscarried. Or *we* miscarried?
    - Us, telling everyone we were actually pregnant before Christmas and lost that one too.
    - Us, dealing with *all that...*
    - Me, learning what happens when a woman miscarries.
    - Me, wondering why I didn't know this before, like in December.
    - Us, arguing.
    - My wife, flushing.
    - Me, hearing the flush.
    - Us, crying.
    - Our son, playing while we did.

- July

  - My wife, telling me about another blue cross.
  - Us, not really excited.
  - Another one of our babies, gone.
  - Another flush.
  - Us, empty.
  - Our son, playing while we were.

- August

  - Us, sitting in "Specialists'" offices.
  - Us, not getting answers.
  - Us, filling out forms.
  - Us, meeting with strangers in cities.
  - Us, accepting apologies.
  - Us, breaking.
  - Us, never smiling.
  - Our son, playing while we tried.

- September

  - Me, getting blood work.
  - Me, wondering why *I* need blood work.
  - My wife, in surgery, DNC, far from home, the big city.
  - Me, waiting; our son, at daycare, back home.
  - Me, driving, leaving, my wife, unconscious, in recovery, nauseated, open, weak, empty, scraped, scared, in pain, picking up our son, playing; me, praying, why? Our son, whining, my wife, away, our life, broken, weak, the test results, pending, my worst day.
  - Us, waiting, for two weeks, longest ever, cancer? Maybe? Dying? Possible? Hearing nothing, getting scared.
  - Me, lost, tempted, confused, driven elsewhere, dark, drinking, lying, crying, silent.
  - Our son; me, not really knowing?
  - Us, Friday, answering the call, the doctor, asking to meet on *Monday?!* Us, pissed about the weekend.
  - Us, waiting for Monday.

- Us, Monday, the front porch, our son, inside with friends, Us, on the phone, the doctor, explaining that we can never have kids again.
- Us, processing...processing...processing...cannot find a connection.

- October–December

  - Us, hurting, me, hating.
  - Us, perfecting our story; HLA-DQA1, Celiac, my DNA + her DNA = ☹, me, fertile, my wife, fertile, us = still fucking fertile, Rheumatoid Arthritis, autoimmune disease?, could've had five daughters, no more babies, no cure, no treatment, very rare, pregnancy = possible, pregnancy = miscarriage, nothing we can do, very rare, ONLY KNOWN TRIGGER = BIRTH OF A HEALTHY BOY.
  - Hormones, needing control.
  - Our bodies, killing our babies.
  - God, killing our babies.
  - Birth, needing control.
  - Us, buying Christmas presents.
  - Our only son, sleeping while we did.
  - New Years, us, living, just.

2017

Healing...

2018

Ibid.

2019

We don't meet Clarence till the end.

When George Bailey hears the bell on his Christmas tree and his daughter, bless her heart, reminds him that every time a bell rings, an angel gets its wings.

Attaboy, Clarence. Roll credits.

It may defy our yuletide nostalgia, but the truth is that for the first 100 min of Frank Capra's cinematic classic, *It's a Wonderful Life* is really just a series of isolated vignettes and seemingly disjointed—and non-Christmassy—anecdotes, the significance of which is only solidified by what comes at the end. Nevertheless, *It's a Wonderful Life* still resonates as the timeless tale of down-on-his-luck George Bailey's chance to see what the world would be like if he had never been born. Before nearly committing suicide by jumping off a frozen bridge on Christmas Eve, George's guardian angel, Clarence, shows our wallowing every-man-hero a harrowing glimpse of the countless lives he's touched and reminds him, through the course of the final act, of the titular message of the iconic Christmas film.

Except the movie really isn't about Christmas at all. And Clarence is hardly in it. Yet, even though the majority of the movie has nothing to do with Christmas, and even though Clarence first appears on screen with just over twenty minutes remaining, the legacy of *It's a Wonderful Life* seems to rest singularly in these waning scenes. The arrival of Clarence—the better angel, perhaps, of George's own nature—solders our forlorn protagonist's otherwise frustratingly stymied circumstance to his revived awareness of the sublime that hides in the mundane. Without Clarence, George's is just another life, neither noteworthy nor necessarily wonderful. Clarence's self-revelation gives meaning to Georgia and his struggle; it alleviates his grieving while maintaining the integrity of the struggle itself. Clarence doesn't save George from anything. His house is still drafty, his uncle, still senile, and his town, still owned, for the most part, by the evil Mr. Potter. The only thing Clarence offers George upon his divine emergence on that bridge is the chance to rise as the champion of his own existence. Therein, upon his acceptance, lies George's greatest victory. It just took him awhile to get there.

But that doesn't mean those first hundred minutes don't matter. We need the plot to get the point. Clarence was always there, of course, watching from the sidelines, talking with God, biding his time before George decides to take a leap of—or maybe, from—faith. He just made sure to make his splash first.

I've never leaned off a bridge on Christmas Eve. Unlike George Bailey, I've never threatened my kid's teacher or assaulted an old man or stormed out of my house on my way to the bar. I've never asked God to keep me from killing myself, and loud bells sometimes hurt my ears. For the first half of my thirties, I hated *It's a Wonderful Life*. I saw too much of myself in the Pre-Clarence George Bailey. A man victimized by the universe, eternally cursed and burdened with rocks and hills and shackles and Gods laughing as I stumble, on repeat. I grew tired of praying for a Clarence that never came, and even though I never leaned off an actual bridge—or ones with three-point spreads, full kegs, jpgs, spread legs, or worse—I started marking them throughout the maps that I made of my world, so that I could steer in the fog.

I knew about gravity and what would happen if I ever jumped out of my life. And I knew that I wouldn't have an angel to drink tea with after. Only kids believe in Santa. But I also knew—or hoped or prayed—that maybe I didn't need one. Santa served a purpose when I was a kid; but I make my own presence now. I can't build another chair for our table for three. I can't write my way back into a high school classroom or theorize a cure for our little DNA problem. I can't pray away my depression. But maybe, as a father, husband, teacher, scholar, and citizen, I can now somehow use the Lack that had defined my last five years to promote, in myself and my students, a new spirit of productive inquiry, possibility, progress, and power. Maybe George didn't need Clarence, after all; maybe he would've hit the water, gotten chilly, and found his way back out. Maybe Clarence never even existed. Maybe George just needed to freeze a little before he realized that life is better when you're dry. It may not always be wonderful, but at least it's warm.

My personal struggles have given purpose to my profession. As an English professor—and more specifically, an English Teacher Educator—I now spend my days helping aspiring high school English teachers negotiate the undeniably harsh and thankless realities of American public schools with their idealistic—and oftentimes unrealistic—passions to change those schools and the lives of the kids therein. I watch my students hide their cries while I shoulder the charge of showing them everything they never want—but need—to see about their chosen career.

What the world of schools looks like without them.

And in their eyes, I often see the same pain and confusion and sense of loss that I must have shown all those years ago in that cold hospital room with those stupid drawings and those toothless grins. "It can't really be like this. I thought that it would be different. But I wanted more. I deserve more. Those poor kids. Poor me. I quit."

I've felt my students' struggles, and I know the fear that they feel as their grips on absolutes and innocence loosen. That stinging feeling of bliss betrayed, when Santa brings the kid next door the toy that you really wanted. The pain of laboring for naught, and the sobering truth that hope alone can't fix broken systems. I empathize with every one of my students when their lesson plans fail. And with every one of their students who curse at them or ignore them or make them feel small, I remember that ultrasound tech and her wand and the beeping and the goo.

It's amazing how similar some jobs are.

A part of me will always want to help my students quit. Find their bridges and give a loving push. Teaching's absurd. Kids are assholes, and parents are worse. And don't get me started with cell-phones. Go make more money doing literally anything else and eat and be happy. Cheers. Maybe George should've just jumped. His world would suffer, but he'd be none the wiser.

But then I see my son. my only. Yup, just him. And I see my wife. The artist, my lover, and best friend. I see all the times that we've had at our table for three and am grateful for all the rest that we have left on our plate. In these moments, something about my life and my job and my kids and my purpose starts to make sense.

Because yes, teaching can suck. It's hard. Thankless and absurd. And sometimes cold, and often lonely. But it's also beautiful. And strong. And our students and their stories and our schools *can be* places of beauty. Of strength and survival. Granted, that beauty doesn't necessarily heat the freezing waters of public education, or the biting sting of a world that insists on hitting you. George Bailey's triumph over his life doesn't make the circumstances of that life any less mediocre. Awareness of suffering doesn't cure suffering, and maybe the harsh truth of any Clarence is that the relativity of *wonder* means that sometimes full lives still lack something.

Still, my experiences over these last few years have somehow allowed me to find heat in that freezing and strength in the fragility of our moment. We don't have to pick between pouty George and pious Clarence. While, yes, we can choose to live as one or the other, maybe true awareness—serenity, transcendence, absurd heroism, or whatever construct you may need to get you through the day—comes from channeling the complex and contradictory virtues of both.

Through our losses, I now bond with my students in ways I never could have imagined if I had five daughters or another wife. My life as a pre-Clarence George has given me the perspective and insights needed to marble my sorrows with those of any student who anguishes over the state of American education: the loss of students that they never had and the crippling torment of worrying that they won't be enough for the ones who'll one day fill their seats.

It's easy to quit. If you look close enough, every map has bridges. If I teach my students anything, though, it's that in order to avoid succumbing to their own inevitable teaching bridges, they must first locate them. Name them. Build shrines around, note the currents, mark the coordinates, and mind their shadows. Maybe even walk out every now and then to check the view and clear the coast. Then get the hell out and keep doing the good well.

Because we don't grieve in order. There's no logic or sequence to pain. Loss goes in cycles, as do gains. Our memories of today may hurt because of what comes tomorrow; later always determines Yesterday's legacy. My grittiest and most promising teachers will fail, even after they've succeeded. I will be there to help them.

Jumping in first to ease their plunge.

Because I've grudged too long worrying about becoming George Bailey, flirting with bridges and waiting for angels to save me. I've flicked off flickering monitors, covered empty wombs, and carried my son to bed while flushes echo down the hall. Yes, for my wife and me, holidays will always taste a little salty, and holding other babies will probably always make us kind of bitter. But there's a comfort in certain, unforced, resignations: a calmness in those churning waters that once drained me, the acrobatics of constraint and the freedom of incompletion. In my absence, I've found gratitude. In my grieving, peace.

I've never written Santa a thank-you note. I should.

Maybe.

Then again, maybe I'll just wait until after the holidays.

Bells still hurt, wings and all.

CHAPTER 14

Reading, Loving, and Losing My Mother: A Collage of Partial Understanding

Brandon Sams

In *Unclaimed Experience,* Caruth (1996) writes, "knowing and not know-ing are entangled in the language of trauma and in the stories associated with it" (p. 4). Traumatic experience "defies and demands our witness" and is represented "in a language that is always somehow literary" (p. 5). The literary—naming as it slips, claiming as it vanishes. In the spirit of Caruth's estimation of trauma, this collage is caught up in knowing and not knowing, even as it attempts utterance in fragments.

* * *

In *Fun Home* (2006), a graphic memoir of her childhood, Alison Bechdel describes an epistemological crisis she suffered at a young age. She recounted her daily activities in writing and how she began litter-ing her work with *I think.* Her perceptions became decidedly only her perceptions, subject to doubt and erasure. Co-emerging with this crisis, she observed that members of her family were emotionally isolated. They

B. Sams (✉)
Iowa State University, Ames, IA, USA
e-mail: blsams@iastate.edu

© The Author(s) 2020
S. A. Shelton and N. Sieben (eds.),
Narratives of Hope and Grief in Higher Education,
https://doi.org/10.1007/978-3-030-42556-2_14

181

invested their energies in art instead of each other. "Our home was like an artists' colony. We ate together, but otherwise were absorbed in our separate pursuits...the more gratification we found in our own geniuses, the more isolated we grew" (p. 134). To counter the loss of parental intimacy, Alison obsessed over what she could control, until even ordinary objects and thoughts tormented her: "my *I thinks* were gossamer sutures in that gaping rift between signifier and signified" (p. 143). Alison's mother, Helen, noticed Alison's anxiety. Instead of rehearsing lines for playacting, she read to Alison during the evenings, a powerful relational act that helped to restore their emotional intimacy and heal Alison's compulsions.

* * *

"Questions without answers must be asked very slowly," Anne Michaels (1996) writes (p. 159). I've been estranged from my mother for 18 years. That's almost half my life. I'm in the habit of asking a lot of questions. How might our lives be different, and how can they not be? Can anything be said or done to reconcile our relationship? Can I reclaim—can *we* reclaim—what's been lost? What *has* been lost? We've met for brief visits only a few times since 2001. We text: me mostly about the Iowa winter, her about work and the Texas summer. I sometimes wonder how an emoji came to represent the depth of our communication.

* * *

Dennis Sumara's (2002) *Why Reading Literature in School Still Matters* is one of the most beautiful academic texts I've ever read. Sumara described relationships to significant objects, including books, being central to the stories we tell ourselves about ourselves. The making of identity depends, in part, on continuous and deliberate interpretation. One of Sumara's arguments was that reading books can be an important act of identity making. He highlighted the special importance that rereading and writing play in the ongoing process of inventing a self. When we return to a frequently read and written in text, we see past versions of ourselves in the margins, an invitation of sorts to interpret not only the literary text anew, but to read past selves and to imagine future ones: the readers we were in relation to the readers we are and might be. Because we have been shaped by history and culture, acts of reading and the literary objects that make those experiences possible serve as personal and cultural archives. Sumara named the literary objects that serve as these archives commonplace books.

* * *

About collage, Peter Elbow advises to "put things together if they sort of go. They need to "go" ... but not too well" (p. 26). Engagement increases where there is some "friction, resistance, difference" (p. 26). I'm hoping, too, that sense can be found in the assemblage. "One can look deeply for meaning or one can invent it,"—Anne Michaels helps me have faith in the assembling itself (1996, p. 136). Refusing to offer a closed and fixed argument, a collage invites the reader to playfully fill in the gaps offered by the text. I'm wondering: What does collage offer the writer?

* * *

The Bible was my first commonplace book. My sacred reading at a young age was sometimes voluntary, sometimes forced, but always performed. Afraid quite literally of going to hell, I prayed without ceasing for Jesus to enter my heart. My repeated requests never gave me the confidence one might expect. My mother's and grandmother's Bibles had been read, written in, worn out—and I wanted mine to look the same. If I was seen reading, then surely, by community vote if nothing else, Jesus would enter my heart.

* * *

I'm in the habit of keeping a daybook—a kind of commonplace book—for my pre-service English education methods courses. I ask students to keep one, too, and feel increasingly out of place making this request because students have access to so much technology to record their thinking. I sometimes think we've forgotten how to pay attention—I'm including myself here—and any attempt at focusing our attention or slowing down will make us uncomfortable. I ask students to use the daybook in familiar ways: to record their thinking about course readings and class discussion, to reflect on observing or teaching in the field, or to write when they feel prompted.

In "Finding Time," Rebecca Solnit (2007) asks us to think of slowness as "an act of resistance, not because slowness is a good in itself but because of all that it makes room for" (para. 10). I like to think that daybook writing—writing by hand in particular—makes room for the "not-yet-thought" by slowing us down, inviting us to take notice of our world in ways that might not be possible in the everyday blur of living. Reading and rereading a daybook, or any commonplace, is an exercise in creative interpretation. One can stitch together a sensible story through fragments.

* * *

I'm connected to my mother and family members through social media. I frequently see their posts at the top of my screen. The mysterious algorithm underlines the gulf between us. Their mixture of far-right politics and religious fundamentalism is hard to miss in my feed of left-leaning and hard left connections. Recently, someone posted a pro-Brett Kavanaugh meme: a photo of two children, a young boy kissing a young girl, with the caption, "in 40 years this will come back to haunt me!" Other posts urge to "Pray for our President" and equate the gates of heaven to the proposed wall on the Southern border. I never comment. Sometimes I stare. Sometimes I show my partner, and we shake our heads, amazed. How did I come from this? How is *this* still with me? I don't unfollow or unfriend my mother or my family. I need to know where I came from. And, in a strange way, reading these posts makes our relationship easier to live with. We're not close enough to fight.

* * *

When I teach "Methods of Teaching Writing" to pre-service English teachers, I often assign a literacy memoir. Each of us carries powerful experiences with reading and writing in and out of school. Whether we realize it or not, these experiences shape our attitudes and perspectives about literacy, including what it means to be a good student and writer, what it means to be a good (writing) teacher. The purpose of the memoir is to remember these experiences—to narrate them in an appealing way, in storied form, and to critically reflect on these experiences through a teacher's lens. I'm amazed at the thoughtful connections students make between their literacy pasts and future literacy teaching.

Students write wonderfully rich stories: about painting alongside Bob Ross to ease writing anxiety; hacking the algorithm of a machine-scored writing placement assessment; struggling with reading and writing because of ADHD. Sometimes—not often, but sometimes—a student will question the role of "the personal" in the assignment, and in academic writing more generally. A few years ago, a student memorably—and somewhat terrifyingly—wrote a fictional piece that critiqued the presumptions of the literacy memoir and the power dynamics at play in the writing classroom. In his fictionalized account, I forced every student to read their work at the front of the room. I mocked his incompetence when he began to read. He peed his pants, underlining my ruthless authority and his shame and humiliation. The memoir was many things, but it seemed primarily to function as a scathing critique of "the personal" in the writing classroom. I assumed that students would want to trust me, and that the literacy memoir was a way to cement that trust—that I would receive the past gently and help them use their stories as a source for learning. I have rarely felt as critiqued and intimidated as a teacher. I try not to think about this student or his memoir, but I do.

* * *

"Maybe college isn't for you." No one in my family had been to college, so everything about it was an unknown quantity. I had a vague sense that it would cost a lot of money, alongside a creeping fear that we couldn't afford it. When I was 17 years old, I enrolled in a dual-credit economics class at the local community college. I got good grades in high school—I was in the running for valedictorian, in fact—but grades were entirely too important to me back then. A bad grade would turn my life upside down. My score on the first economics exam caused seismic panic: I scored a 72. I had never made a C in my life. I broke down in front of my mother, inconsolable. My first college test, a possible precursor for what college would really be like, and I had failed miserably. My high school experience—my entire world up to that point—felt small.

* * *

"Maybe college isn't for you." It stung then and still stings a little bit. I'd built up an identity centered on being smart, and Mom punctured everything with what felt like an impossible truth. Maybe college wasn't for me. I went back to economics class unsure if I'd persist. The professor told us that he had created two versions of the exam and that the wrong grading key had been applied to some. Mine was one of them. I got my corrected exam back two days later: I scored 107.

Mom was relieved when I told her. I was relieved too. But she still said it, and I continue to wonder why. Maybe she was trying to save me from pretending to be someone I'm not. Maybe she was trying to save me money and toil. Maybe she was afraid of where I'd go and who I might become.

* * *

I don't read the Bible much. I've spent my life moving away. Reading and writing have given me new ideas, identities, and communities and, perhaps, have helped dilute the strength of those first books and places of learning. Try as I may to read and write my way out of the past, I read and write my way back in.

* * *

Fun Home (2006) is a wonderful example of intertextuality and the intertextual character of life writing. In her memoir, Bechdel attended to the life and death of her father, Bruce, including his closeted identity as a gay man, and how his life and their relationship shaped, constrained, and made hers (im)possible. After her father's death—a suspected suicide— Alison and her partner, Joan, go home to visit her mother, Helen. There's a poignant scene in the family library, a space that represents Bruce's emotional and aesthetic retreat to the art and lives of others, where Helen invites Joan to select any volume for her own. She picks a book of Wallace Stevens' poetry. Thrilled at their mutual love of Stevens, Helen turns to "Sunday Morning," a poem about the crucifixion of Jesus. After hearing Helen read a few fragments aloud, including Stevens' reference to the crucifixion as "the old catastrophe" (p. 55), Alison begins making reflective connections between Stevens' poem, the crucifixion, and her parents' relationship.

> Perhaps she [Helen] also liked the poem because its juxtaposition of catastrophe with a plush domestic interior is life with my father in a nutshell. Dad's death was not a new catastrophe but an old one that had been unfolding very slowly for a long time. (p. 83)

Helen's slow dismantling of Bruce's library is both a literal and symbolic deconstruction of artifice, of Bruce's means of emotional and literal

retreat. Yet, Alison's project of making sense of her life is inextricably connected to her father and her father's literary practices. He is both midwife
and obstacle. Perhaps the act of naming the catastrophe as such serves as
Alison's agentive act of being and living otherwise within a complicated
and continuous intertext. Naming is her leap of faith and act of love—to
understand more deeply the relationships, places, and objects that shape
her identity.

* * *

In *Teaching Queer* (2017), Stacey Waite ruminated on the names of
things. Whether naming parts of speech, elements of writing, or identities, the act of naming can flatten complications and reify normative
orders and hierarchies. What happens when the names of things fail us?
What happens when language fails to convey what we want to say or who
we are or have become? "I remember that for queer bodies, names are
a matter of survival. If there are not new and shifting names, I myself
as a genderqueer teacher of this class cease to exist as myself" (p. 61).
Renaming is survival, becoming, becoming otherwise.

* * *

When I was a child, my mother bought me a picture book with birds:
cardinal, blue jay, robin. I spent hours looking at the pictures and names.
My mother took my hand and helped me trace the letters. I uttered names
of birds and pointed to the trees, to the sky, whenever I had a chance.
I've learned from my mother's humorous recounting that "Card-bird"
was one of my first and favorite words. A few years ago, my mother sent
me a new copy of the picture book—perhaps to remind me where and
how I first learned the names of things, and who was there to support my
efforts.

REFERENCES

Bechdel, A. (2006). *Fun home: A family tragicomic*. Boston, MA: Mariner Books.
Caruth, C. (1996). *Unclaimed experience: Trauma, narrative, and history*. Balti-
more, MD: Johns Hopkins University Press.
Elbow, P. (1998). Collage: Your cheatin' art. *Writing on the Edge, 9*(1), 26–40.
Michaels, A. (1996). *Fugitive pieces: A novel*. New York, NY: Vintage Interna-
tional.

Solnit, R. (2007). Finding time. *Orion Magazine*. Retrieved from https://orionmagazine.org/article/a-fistful-of-time/.

Sumara, D. (2002). *Why reading literature in school still matters: Imagination, interpretation, insight*. Mahwah, NJ: Lawrence Erlbaum.

Waite, S. (2017). *Teaching queer: Radical possibilities for writing and knowing*. Pittsburgh, PA: University of Pittsburgh Press.

CHAPTER 15

Love You to pIeCEs

Lyndsey Nunes

On August 1, 2017, at approximately 1:42 PM, I hung up the phone with Randi, one of my most promising mentees. I was supposed to call her back on my way back to campus but got sidetracked. I didn't think twice about not calling back. We had dinner plans the next night, and she knew that I was distracted with personal issues that she had described as "a shitstorm of a summer." We planned to continue talking about life, her five teaching job offers, and graduate school at dinner. That dinner did not happen and never will. Less than 17 hours later, I was hanging up the phone again, this time with her mother who called to tell me that Randi had died. She had died by suicide. The shock of the news still overwhelms me. I know what I was wearing, where I stood in my house as I fell to the floor to bury my face in my hands, gasping for breath while my phone lay beside me on the floor, as her mom's tears echoed through the speaker. In that moment I kept thinking it was a car accident, murder—anything but suicide. Suicide didn't make sense, and most days it still doesn't. What Randi described as a shitstorm of a summer had become unimaginably worse.

L. Nunes (✉)
Westfield State University, Westfield, MA, USA

© The Author(s) 2020
S. A. Shelton and N. Sieben (eds.),
Narratives of Hope and Grief in Higher Education,
https://doi.org/10.1007/978-3-030-42556-2_15

189

I constantly replay our last conversation, wondering what I missed. Death by suicide leaves survivors with many unanswered burning questions like, "If I had called her back, could I have changed this?" A suicide survivor tends to blame themselves while trying to understand their loved one's decision, wondering, "How could I have prevented it? How did I fail her? What could I have done?" For me, I constantly wonder, "Did I fail her family? They trusted me as her mentor. Did I fail her friends, my other students, some mentees themselves?" Immediately following Randi's death, I was the one they were all turning to for help and answers that I didn't have. I felt helpless. I didn't know what to do for or say to them. I felt numb, confused, and a failure. I felt immense levels of guilt, and most days I still do.

Randi was the motivated, confident, mature, and compassionate valedictorian at our university. She had a smile that lit up a room and a contagious laugh that you would see or hear as she wheeled by on-campus on her blue light-up scooter. She excelled at everything she did, always making it look easy. She was committed to her academics, extracurriculars, her family and friends. Being her mentor gave me immeasurable pride. Now in hindsight, I wonder if her ability to flawlessly excel was what blinded me to her inner battles. Maybe perfection with a smile was her warning sign, and hiding her darkness was the ultimate demonstration of her brilliance. I will never know what happened in the hours between our last conversation and her final decision. Could a returned phone call have saved her? In my attempts to heal and to release my guilt, I have told myself that it wouldn't have. I know I can't live in the past or the what-ifs, but it's impossible not to.

Randi died one month before the start of the semester. As the semester began, I found myself spinning in a world that knew her and wasn't prepared to answer questions or provide clarity. I felt a tremendous responsibility to care for all of Randi's friends. I needed to help them cry, laugh, and try to understand something that I personally couldn't. Maybe I put that pressure on myself as a way to make up for feeling responsible for not taking care of her, or maybe it was from the environment in which I was grieving; either way, it added an additional level of complexity to my grief and healing that I was trying to navigate. I had to teach myself to not overanalyze student interactions. I was consumed with worry that every excelling student was secretly struggling and was going to die. We learn about common depression and suicidal warning signs, like changes in mood, withdrawal, unusual or impulsive behaviors, dangerous behaviors, or extreme hopelessness (Leming & Dickinson, 2016). But what about those who are depressed and aren't exhibiting these observable behaviors? Hyper alertness and personal fear changed how I interacted with everyone. Initially, I emotionally shut myself in, only surrounding myself with those who knew Randi. I could not bear to make connections with new students. My friends and family didn't understand, and most days I didn't either. I kept moving small steps forward, trying to find moments of strength by living life honoring Randi's legacy: proudly wearing tie-dye and organizing events in her name to make the world a more inclusive place. This process was slow, but with every interaction, I found more hope and strength.

HOPE

Gently, I began changing my approach to life. I found that by sharing my own story I was able to provide insight, support, guidance, and encouragement. It should be noted that this is my story, a single story, of how when faced with a life tragedy, I found hope in my grieving. Hope looks different for everyone, but the idea of it is a state that many strive for during their grieving process. For me, hope is a state of being or a feeling that you know that no matter what adversity that you face, things will get better. Hope is made up of both actions and thoughts that influence each other. It's pushing myself forward in challenging times, doing the little things I need to do to keep myself going. I try to feel the ups and downs of the situations because I can't live in a fake place of hope; I need to let myself get knocked down and feel it. But then, its hope that eventually picks me back up. Thoughts of a better future and remembering my past experiences remind me that I will be okay and gives me glimmers of hope.

Looking back at what you've been through and sharing your story with others can be a part of someone people's survival guide. It was for me. As I began navigating my new life, I read books and listened to podcasts of people living in worlds of grief and pain. Through my own grieving process, I found the importance of being a voice—one that needed to be heard, one that could address suicide prevention and awareness. The finale song of Act 2 of the musical *Hamilton* is "Who lives, who dies, who tells your story?" (Miranda, 2015). These words, which are repeated throughout the song, speak to me, and my relationship with Randi. These words support my attempt to find hope and healing through my grieving, by continuing to live a life that carries on Randi's legacy. Randi was going to change the world. I hope that by sharing our story, her legacy will continue to promote an inclusive and accepting world. On my darkest days, I think about all of the positive things being done in her honor: an accessible playground, a scholarship for education majors, fundraisers for the American Foundation for Suicide Prevention (AFSP). Thinking about these things brings color to my world when I need it most, just like Randi did.

MENTOR

The word *mentor* is loosely explained as an experienced and trusted advisor, from whom you aspire to learn (Eby, Rhodes, & Allen, 2007). Immediately following the loss of Randi, colleagues referred to her as my mentee. I hadn't given our relationship that label while she was on campus, even though she regularly sought out my counsel, attended conferences with me, and used me as an advisor. She wasn't just my mentee though; she was also my friend. I have spent time conceptualizing the definitions of mentee and mentor in relation to Randi and me. Eby et al. (2007) suggested that a mentor is different from a role model and observer, teacher and student, or advisor and advisee. Based on my experience in academia, I agree that the teacher/student and advisor/advisee relationships are different from mentoring. A prime example is as an advisor telling an advisee what classes that they need for degree requirements, but not serving in any other role. I define a mentor as an experienced individual who is a role model in both professional and personal areas; someone who, while learning alongside, provides support and direction, challenges mentees to learn and grow, and advises mentees. The extent to which mentoring relationships are positive or negative is rooted in the mentor and mentee personality characteristics. There is a higher likelihood for a more successful mentorship if the mentee trusts the mentor and develops a deeper reciprocal relationship. Reciprocity is key. The mentor will learn from the mentee, and they grow together. In my mentor-mentee relationship with Randi, I refined my mentor abilities based on our interactions. I trusted her abilities and provided her with opportunities for success and failure; in return, I trusted myself to support her. I have since wondered if the relationship we developed, as open, honest, and trusting as it was, was actually a negative outcome relative to her not wanting to share with me her internal battles, for the fear of disappointing me.

Relationship emphasis is a mentoring dimension that requires mentors to exhibit a genuine acceptance of the student's feelings (Cohen & Galbraith, 1995). If we don't know their true feelings, then how do we genuinely accept them? I would joke with Randi and her peers that I knew too much about them and didn't need the intimate details. I knew about their love lives, breakups, friendships, social activities, etc. Randi, following a breakup, came to me distraught, expressing deep emotions. She was always honest, not just in these moments, but in general when expressing her thoughts and feelings. So, I struggle with processing those moments; I wonder if what I felt were her deep emotions were actually just the tip of an iceberg of a very dark, cold place.

As mentors, we are rarely qualified or equipped to understand or safely support these true feelings. Mentors are not counselors; we are advisors, and it is important to remember this distinction. Had Randi shared with me what she was actually feeling, I don't know that I would have known what to say or do. I try to think that I would have saved her life; I would have hopefully done everything right, but I'm not sure. I don't know that I would have. This is where the guilt of not being given the chance to *try* sets in. Then, I'm not sure what I would rather have: no chance at all to help or having the chance but also having same outcome. Most likely the latter. I question almost daily why she didn't say anything to anyone. I worry about how this could relate to other students. Are students purposefully hiding their feelings from us? Is it because they're trying to make sense of their feelings themselves, trying to find the words to express them? Could they be ashamed and don't want to look weak or feel they're disappointing us? Did she hide it because she was so exceptional and worried that we might think less of her? There are still and will always be so many lingering questions, with little chance of answers.

NOTES

Randi was one of the founding members of the club pIeCEs, which stands for Positive Inclusion of Everyone Creates Educational Success. The ICE was capitalized to recognize the name of the dual-enrollment program that I coordinate, the Inclusive Concurrent Enrollment Initiative Program. pIeCEs provides individuals with intellectual disabilities authentically inclusive college experiences, specifically social experiences. The club is one of the main reasons for the success of our program. We, students and staff, pride ourselves on constantly exchanging the club slogan, "Love you too pIeCEs," with one another. We feel that it highlights our diverse lives, that we are all made of different pIeCEs, and by saying it, we show that we love every one of those different pIeCEs, no matter what, and would do anything to help each other.

At the time when I was finishing this manuscript, Randi had been dead for a year and half. A year and a half with no note, no answers or closure, but lots of guilt and confusion. A colleague told me that when a note is found, it doesn't always provide closure; it might not answer questions and might even leave you with more. My colleague was right. As I was wrapping up my writing, Randi's mother gave me Randi's computer in hopes to incorporate Randi's own words into our story. I found more than that. I found suicide notes that she had hidden away. Notes are written to those she loved and trusted, me being one of them. They were filled with loving apologies as she said good-bye. She begged us not to blame ourselves, told us that there was nothing that we could have done, and that she was purposefully hiding these dark demons. She wrote that we were there through the highs, the lows, and the in-between. She wrote "I love you too pIeCEs." A phrase that had once been something exchanged on the regular between many of us now held an even deeper, incomprehensible meaning. I still grapple with the fact that, as much as she loved and trusted us, she didn't trust us enough to help with her pIeCEs that were in pain. And the only way to stop it was suicide.

The pain and suicidal thoughts that Randi was feeling didn't rear their heads for the first time on August 1. She had been fighting the darkness for some time; she had written the notes two months before taking her life. During those two months, I had talked to her almost every day. She was checking-in daily with a simple text or a funny meme, always trying to make me smile, all while finding the will to continue living. I was grieving a miscarriage that co-occurred with my partner being diagnosed with a chronic autoimmune disease that resulted in paralysis. I had just finished my Ph.D. and was ready for the next chapter of my life, but instead found the life that I had planned slipping away. During these months, Randi was helping me, when I should have been helping her. While we talked daily, looking back, I feel like it was one-sided because I was grieving and lost in my own world. I wonder if helping me was a way for her to focus on others' versus her own sadness, or if maybe she was giving me everything she could, because she knew then that she wouldn't be here in the future to do so. Had there been a sign of her internal battle, I would have spent two months trying to put her pIeCEs back together. For the first time in 18 months, I was angry—so angry with her and myself. I felt selfish that I was so absorbed with my life, and that might have been why I had missed a sign. I was angry beyond belief, and then I wasn't. I wasn't because I went back to her not wanting us to know she was hurting. She said this herself. My colleague was right: I do have more questions. Why didn't she trust me to help? She seemed emotionally aware of her state; it was evident in the clarity of her notes. I've worried if, because of that relationship we had built, she didn't want to fall off the pedestal that I put her on. I've spent hours searching her computer and haven't found any more answers, but what I have found is that death by suicide is a soul-crushing experience that hurts—hurts more than words can explain.

SUICIDE

Suicide. A taboo word, an untouched topic resulting in mixed attitudes that people don't readily/easily discuss. It's a topic I rarely found myself talking about, never mind even thinking about. That has changed since losing Randi. My behavior analyst mind needed to know why it happened, and in trying to make sense of her loss, I dove headfirst into all the information I could find: books, movies, blogs, support groups, etc. I thought that death by suicide was uncommon, but I was wrong; it's actually becoming more common, as the rate of suicide has steadily increased over the last 10 years. It is the tenth leading cause of death in the United States, and the second leading cause of death of individuals between the ages of 18–24, the average age of undergraduate students (American Foundation for Suicide Prevention, 2019). Suicide survivors often refrain from talking about their losses, which can be a result of the stigma surrounding suicide. People automatically assume mental health issues when someone dies by suicide, when many people who die by suicide have no diagnosed mental health conditions. Mental health plays a role, but it is not the whole story.

Talk saves lives. As I have said, I hope that by sharing our story, my now-suicide-survivor experience, that narrative might help someone else. I'm a runner and know how important physical health is, but mental health is just as important—sometimes more so. We need to normalize the mental health conversation by raising awareness and switching the focus to suicide as a preventable health outcome. We need to increase mental health literacy to teach people to recognize possible signs of someone struggling and have knowledge of available resources that can direct people to help.

I've participated in trainings where I've been taught what *typical* or *normal* depression or suicidal ideation warning signs to be aware of in students. None of these fairly short trainings prepared me for Randi. I was looking for the withdrawn student making hopeless comments, not the valedictorian accepting her first job. Randi exhibited none of these; she was planning her future, buying things for her classroom, lesson planning. She had even written her welcome letter to her future class and their families. The lack of warning signs is more common than not (Leming & Dickinson, 2016). This is why it is critical that people expand their understandings of suicide and mental health. It's important that we get more than the usual information; we need different information. This could include, but is not limited to, information about anxiety and depression, preventative strategies, research about suicide, college student risk factors, and mental health awareness. One in five people has some type of mental health diagnosis, and not all will result in suicide, but in a class of 20 students there are likely at least four who are struggling in some way. I think that we should be offered opportunities to broaden our knowledge and to learn ways to embed preventative measures within our teaching.

The lack of warning signs is terrifying because, how do we help if we don't know someone needs it? Why would we ask questions or worry about people, if we think that they are fine? Especially when there might be others behaving in ways telling us that they need help? It's a hard place to be in, this state of hypersensitivity and alertness that every student could possibly die by suicide. I've found that if I ask the questions that I need to, that I am prepared to listen but also have knowledge about the next step—which doesn't mean that I have to be the one to provide the services; it's directing them to the necessary resources.

As mentors, we have opportunities to build trusting and powerful relationships with students by allowing the extra moment to check-in. If you are worried about a student, ask if they might harm themselves. People, like I once did, often worry that by asking something like, "Are you planning to harm yourself?" increases the likelihood of suicidal behaviors. Research actually shows that the expression of care can reduce suicidal feelings (Mathias et al., 2012). This is an example of the different sort of information that we need to be given. I truly don't know if I would have known how to ask Randi if she was contemplating self-harm, because I wouldn't have wanted to give her the idea. Now that I know about the research, I will ask. I've spoken with many colleagues, who admit to being afraid to ask the questions.

A colleague shared a story of a time when she was almost too late to help. She said that while the student did not complete the act, the colleague still carries immense guilt that she missed something; this is something that I know too well. Guilt will consume you; and though unhealthy, it is especially normal after a suicide loss. We need to find ways to forgive ourselves and those we lose. Healing encompasses forgiveness; it is a sign of strength, not weakness. There are documented health benefits when we forgive, such as decreases in anxiety and depression (Swartz, 2018). As I began allowing myself to release the guilt and to forgive myself for not being able to save Randi, I felt my depression lessening, and this gave me little pieces of hope to hold onto. I was finding a way to bring myself out of the dark through forgiveness.

Grief is a complex. It is both an emotion that foments feelings of helplessness and a complex coping process that requires invested energy, in order to address challenges and opportunities (Leming & Dickinson, 2016). We are taught that grief is a negative emotion that has diverse physical, emotional, and social impacts. I have found that grief can actually be positive. It forced me to find hope and joy in unimaginable moments, resulting in commitments to make meaningful life changes, and I'm so thankful. I think that, in a way, grief is necessary to understand what hope means to as a person. I don't think that I would truly understand the concept of hope in relation to my own life, had I not lost Randi when and how I did. I think that if we let ourselves see that positive in grief, it can greatly impact the ways that we as a society respond to suicide.

Grief is a natural response to losing a loved one. As time passes, the majority of people's intense feelings typically decrease as they learn to live without the deceased. Most people experience normal and nonpathological grief known as uncomplicated grief. Complicated grief, experienced by 7% of people, is persistent and traumatic, resulting in an inability to accept loss. The percentage is thought to be higher with those bereaved by suicide (Linde, Treml, Steinig, Nagl, & Kersting, 2017). Unfortunately, research is limited in examining suicide survivor's grief and specifically in exploring complicated grief. This lack is troubling, considering the stigma and needs of suicide survivors.

Linde et al. (2017) conducted a systematic review of grief interventions for suicide survivors. This review only included seven intervention studies, a limitation that speaks volumes about the lack of suicide grief interventions research. Five studies included participants who were immediate family—child, parent, or spouses. Two of the studies identified participants as *other*. I hypothesize that this other is an unrecognized griever, a person outside of an immediate family—which is where I fall with Randi.

Leming and Dickinson (2016) explained the concept of disenfranchised grief for unrecognized grievers. The social sanctions and lack of empathy for unrecognized grievers are illuminated by the differences in wakes and funerals. Wakes are often during after-work hours, and draw larger crowds, while funerals are usually during the day with less attendees. One explanation of larger wake attendance is because work is less likely to provide employees with time off for non-family deaths. This essentially sets a standard that people are only able to grieve for family within certain time limits or within certain relationships. Truthfully, no one should dictate someone's grieving time based on their perception of a relationship. We all feel things differently. Our perceptions in understanding relationships correlate with the empathy that we show one another. When we understand something as a relationship, we are more apt to respect it. I had someone say "If I were you, I would have been over that girl dying in three days. I would have been mad and realized it was what it was and just moved on." That girl? She has a name: Randi. Three days? I wish. Mad or angry? Not with her, just myself. I wonder, if Randi and I had had a more understandable relationship like her being a little sister, if their response to me would have been the same?

Understanding Me

I'm an extremely self-reflective person diagnosed with ADHD, who over-analyzes every behavior and thought. Overanalyzing is my greatest strength and my greatest weakness. Some days, I'm amazed by my ability to hyperfocus on one thing while shutting out other things for days, months, even years. I spend hours perseverating on my behaviors in order to identify their functions. I had an interesting childhood, full of life experiences that taught me to laugh in the moment, smile my way through, and assure everyone that life is fine. Doing so is much easier than saying what was always on my mind. Most describe me as an extremely empathetic person, full of passionate emotions, and overscheduled to a fault.

I would agree with this description but explain that my overscheduling is how I taught myself to cope. And, I'm rather good at it. I'm able to preoccupy myself with present tasks as a way to not have to directly address deeper-rooted issues. I know that the busier I am, the more that I am running from a situation. Subconsciously, I'm processing, pulling out all the details that require immediate attention and storing away the minor details for another day. This coping strategy supported me through life's ups and downs, while I successfully earned my bachelor's degree, two masters degrees, and a Ph.D. The loss of Randi left me in a much different place.

Immediately after the loss, I stayed busy; I knew I needed to if I was ever going to heal. I followed through on previous commitments, accepted new ones, and found many events to plan in the spare time that I didn't have. My plate was beyond full, and normally this would have helped. About six months in, I realized it wasn't helping. I was beyond processing; I was going through the motions of life, but something was disturbingly wrong. I wasn't there. My mind wasn't there. Literally gone. I was having severe memory issues and had lost my ability to express appropriate emotions. I would be standing in front of classes and forget answers to questions, forget content that I could rattle off in my sleep. This was terrifying. I thought that I was losing it, and thanks to the Internet, I diagnosed myself with early-onset dementia.

As I have said, Randi did not show any typical signs of depression. The media paints depression as someone who is sad, gloomy, and in bed all day. That wasn't Randi, and what I soon found out was that that wasn't me. I was diagnosed with depression and told that my memory loss was a collateral side effect. I was angry. I was short-fused. I was barely sleeping, or sleeping so hard that I wouldn't know the day or month when I woke. The girl who laughed her way through everything with a smile on her face was depressed. I immediately panicked, wondering what this meant for how I would help others, would work, or would work toward my future. I felt like I was in a fish tank with everyone watching me, trying to make it through my days. No one actually knew the extent of my struggles.

The awareness of my memory issues and roller coaster of emotions was petrifying, while at the same time beautiful. When I was forgetting things, I wasn't aware of the depressed reality that I was living in—a reality without Randi. This reality would come crashing down, and I would remember that she was dead. As challenging as it was, the coaster of emotions made me feel alive; they made me feel me again. I began learning things about myself that I had never imagined. As time continued, my self-reflection and weekly therapist visits changed me from hiding my scary reality to talking about it. I was open and honest with family, friends, colleagues, and my students within reason. I didn't overshare but shared enough to let them know that I was human, I was struggling, I needed help, but that I would be okay. One time I said something to one of my classes after I completely forgot that they had a quiz that I had even prepped. After class, a student came up and thanked me. They said that in my being open, they realized that they weren't alone in their own struggles. I found hope through healing, by being a voice.

I started to understand that grief was an active coping process, and as I was healing and grieving, I found a new perspective in life and my abilities. Grief and my response to it made me slow down; it gave me no choice. It made me evaluate who I was and what I needed to do, to be the best version of myself I could be. Slowing down also meant time to focus on what I was experiencing and on research to find out that I wasn't alone. Other suicide survivors had similar experiences and emotions.

Grief can hit you like waves, and these waves can quickly send you back into dark places. The night that I found Randi's notes, it was as if I was reliving learning that she had died. I fell to the floor and laid there crying for what seemed like hours. I was in shock and disbelief. I kept rereading everything. I didn't sleep. The next morning was the start of the semester. Things felt all too similar, except that no one knew that I had the notes. Within a week, the thought of being social made me physically ill. My sleeping was erratic. My emotions were void in moments when they were needed. This time though, knowing that I had been here before and had persevered gave me hope. Experiencing grief taught me to hope; grief, in a weird way, actually became the light that I needed at the end of the tunnel.

This personal experience of losing Randi solidified for me the responsibility that college faculty and staff have to address the importance of mental health awareness and the increasing suicide rates. In higher education, we are lucky to make an impression on the next generation of educators, nurses, law enforcement, or business owners. Let us use this opportunity to directly and indirectly address suicide prevention by providing education and supports to students who may one day need to be a voice themselves. As we are preparing students for their transitions into adulthood, we need to cultivate their levels of grit and resilience by challenging them and assisting them to develop their toolboxes of problem-solving strategies. Often, people want to choose the easier solution because it requires less work, and the right solution to a problem isn't always the easy solution.

High levels of resiliency allow an individual to navigate the uncomfortable while pushing forward. Resiliency, which is when people have the ability to endure hardships and continue on with life, is vital. Resiliency is possible when people have a deep passion or internal drive that people will persevere and progress toward goals. Resiliency is necessary during the problem-solving process. The solution to the problem might not be easy; it could be easier to give up, but the person needs to continue forward. Resiliency provides a solid foundation for the problem-solving process.

We need to expect and allow our students to make mistakes, and we need to be there to support them through their decision-making. Suicide is connected to brain functions that affect decision-making and behavioral control, making it difficult for people to find positive solutions in their given current situations (American Foundation for Suicide Prevention, 2019). No one learns without making mistakes, but how we respond to a mistake and move on is also important. If we are truly effective mentors, then maybe we need to humanize ourselves and let mentees see us make mistakes, struggle, and grieve—even let them be the ones to help us. Maybe, just maybe these are the greatest lessons that we can teach them: It's okay to hurt, it's okay to struggle, it's okay to grieve, but what is important is having hope to continue forward and heal.

While I've made recommendations throughout this chapter, consider this my ultimate one: Tell your story and be a voice. There is great power in storytelling; it makes us memorable and relatable. Tell your stories framed with a purpose, filled with emotions, and filled with messages of hope. The purpose of my story is to lessen a stigma, normalizing suicide survivor's experiences and bringing a needed conversation to a forefront. Suicide survivors may find a nonjudgmental and understanding community in other suicide survivors. While every experience is completely different from another, there are two common threads: a loss to suicide and a struggle with mental health. We need to communicate these stories outside our understanding community. Through storytelling, we can make positive changes in the world, save lives, and bring hope to those affected by suicide. There is no handbook for grief or for life. We all handle things differently, but that variability, our different pIeCEs, is what makes us human. We might not understand one another, but it is important to respect one another and to be willing to use all opportunities, even the difficult ones like experiencing a loss, to learn more about ourselves.

Randi was always teaching everyone, even me as her mentor; it came naturally to her. I truly feel that there is no better example of her ability to teach than what others and I have learned from her loss. Everyone has gone through something that has changed them in an irreversible way. This chapter is a candid and honest exploration into what it meant for me to confront and grieve, but it is only a small peek into my own messy metamorphosis, which has evolved over the last 18 months.

I will never be who I was prior to losing Randi, and I'm okay with that. I've grown to love the new me, who is an advocate, a voice, and a person driven to raise awareness about suicide prevention—in hopes of helping those affected by suicide. This is my single story that I'm sharing, not a know-it-all story. It is a way to help others and also a way to continue healing. I know that there is no clean, perfect ending that I can tie this chapter up with because truthfully, life is messy. Life will be difficult, and there will be dark, stormy days. While I want to say that in those times, we should always find positives, the truth is that that might not always be possible. And that is okay.

Randi loved rainbows and bright colors; it's something we had in common. So, I would feel as if I wasn't fully capturing her if I didn't bring in a rainbow reference. I hope my story reminds you that even during those dark stormy days, there might be the tiniest glimmer of a rainbow in the far corner of your eye; and if you see it, that it reminds you to hope. Understanding your own meaning of hope is vital to your own healing and to moving forward. It doesn't happen overnight, and there will be times when hope is the last thing that you think that you have. But again, that is okay, because you will find it—something which I never thought possible, until I did. One of the last things that Randi said in her letters was to "be kind to people." So, I will leave you with this, as you continue forward in your own story: Be kind to others, but most importantly kind to yourself; you deserve it.

REFERENCES

American Foundation for Suicide Prevention. (2019). *You can fight suicide.* Retrieved from https://afsp.org/.

Cohen, N. H., & Galbraith, M. W. (1995). Mentoring in the learning society. *New Directions for Adult & Continuing Education, 1995*(66), 5–14.

Eby, L. T., Rhodes, J. E., & Allen, T. D. (2007). Definition and evolution of mentoring. In T. D. Allen & L. T. Eby (Eds.), *The Blackwell handbook of mentoring: A multiple perspectives approach* (pp. 7–20). Malden, MA: Blackwell.

Leming, M. R., & Dickinson, G. E. (2016). *Understanding dying, death, & bereavement*. Stamford, CT: Cengage.

Linde, K., Treml, J., Steinig, J., Nagl, M., & Kersting, A. (2017). Grief interventions for people bereaved by suicide: A systematic review. *PLoS One, 12*(6). https://doi.org/10.1371/journal.pone.0179496.

Mathias, C. W., Michael Furr, R., Sheftall, A. H., Hill-Kapturczak, N., Crum, P., & Dougherty, D. M. (2012). What's the harm in asking about suicidal ideation? *Suicide and Life-Threatening Behavior, 42*(3), 341–351.

Miranda, L. (2015). *Hamilton: An American musical* [MP3]. New York: Atlantic Records.

Swartz, K. (2018). *Forgiveness: Your health depends on it*. Retrieved from https://www.hopkinsmedicine.org/health/healthy_aging/healthy_connections/forgiveness-your-health-depends-on-it.

CHAPTER 16

Hope: The Spark of Perseverance to Survive in the Face of Adversity

Nicole DuBois-Grabkowitz

In the summer of 2002, my mother, Margie DuBois, began to have difficulty breathing. Her gait gradually slowed from brisk and purposeful to exaggerated and awkward. Over the course of a year, Margie began climbing the stairs with both her hands and her feet, and she could no longer get out of a chair unaided. Lifting a glass of water to her parched lips became an arduous task, so she would often forgo it altogether, becoming severely dehydrated. Her skin, once a beautiful shade of olive, turned red and flakey, sloughing off to reveal gaping wounds that oozed clear fluid. These wounds would then turn purple and crusty, only to be torn open again to reveal more ooze; she looked as though she had been severely abused. Something was incredibly wrong, but little did we know, the battle for Margie's survival was just beginning.

The onset of Margie's symptoms began around the same time as my maternal grandmother's passing. Margie's apparent lack of desire to move, or even eat, during this time of grief appeared to my father,

N. DuBois-Grabkowitz (✉)
SUNY Old Westbury, Old Westbury, NY, USA

© The Author(s) 2020
S. A. Shelton and N. Sieben (eds.),
Narratives of Hope and Grief in Higher Education,
https://doi.org/10.1007/978-3-030-42556-2_16

205

brother, and even to me to be a normal mourning process. As my grand-mother's primary caretaker, the two were incredibly close and spent large amounts of time together every day; her lack of interest during this time of bereavement seemed to make sense. "Many grievers do experience some very common responses," including periods of "reduced concen-tration, a sense of numbness, disrupted sleep patterns, changed eating habits, and a roller coaster of emotional energy" (James & Friedman, 2009, pp. 13–14). Within the constructs of our society, major loss is so infrequently discussed that we are ill-equipped to handle significant grief events. When a significant grief event does occur, social decorum often dictates that we be left to our own devices to heal. For my mother, it's not that we weren't there for her while she grieved; she preferred to mourn privately and would put on a brave face for the rest of us. It was this ability to stay strong in the face of adversity, this devastating grief over the loss of her mother, coupled with hope, that later helped Margie make significant strides in her journey for wellness.

As time went on, it became increasingly more difficult for Margie to breathe. Her leg muscles were so weak that she was constantly in need of monitoring, to avoid falling or serious injury. Her lesions spread to her face—it was swollen, blotchy, and purple. My mother was nearly unrecog-nizable. We knew that she urgently needed help, but did not know what specialist to contact, so we hoped a general practitioner could guide us. However, as soon as general practitioners learned that my mother had once been a smoker when younger, they dismissed her symptoms alto-gether and provided no guidance. Margie was repeatedly told that her difficulty with breathing was a buildup of fluid in her lungs, "Emphy-sema," they said. And that it would not be long before she succumbed to it. Doctors interpreted her blistering rash as aggressive psoriasis and were unconcerned. "I was so tired all the time; it was very unlike me. And my psoriasis had never been that bad before. Something was different, and very wrong. I couldn't understand why they wouldn't take me seriously" (M. DuBois, personal communication, February 3, 2019). Nearly every physician viewed her exhaustion as laziness, never realizing this was a key symptom for her underlying disease.

As her medical proxy, I vividly recalled one doctor coldly informing my mother that it was only a matter of time before she would suffocate in her own fluids, and that she deserved to die from emphysema as punishment for having been a former smoker.

That cut deep—that doctor meant to hurt my feelings. But I just looked at him, smiled, and replied, "Then you're just not the right doctor for me." Never let people like that have the satisfaction of getting to you, always stay positive. There's always hope, even when others tell you there isn't. Don't ever give up. (M. DuBois, personal communication, February 3, 2019)

Margie always held her head high. "Hope…was primarily a way of thinking, with feelings playing an important, albeit contributory, role" (Snyder, 2002, p. 249). Margie never gave up hope, despite numerous doctors' negativity; she advocated for herself and her family fiercely, as did we for her. This lovingness we shared, this "'armed love,' the fighting love of those convinced of the right and duty to fight, to denounce, and to announce" is what motivated Margie most of all (Freire, 2005, p. 74). We needed her as much as she needed us, and we would do anything to save her.

By October 2002, we still had not gained any traction to identify her mysterious illness. Her symptoms had progressed more aggressively: Margie's breathing was increasingly labored, and she now had dysphagia, meaning that she could no longer swallow food or water. Time was against us; she could not live long without learning how to combat this disease. We later learned that "often an initial complaint is fatigue rather than specific weakness" and that "dysphagia may be associated with a poor prognosis," which meant that Margie was at the end stages of her illness and would be considered terminal (Trüeb, 2001, p. 71). Yet, Margie's hope for finding the right doctor persisted. My brother and I planned out a course of action with her to make this hope become reality.

Desperate for answers, my brother and I laid her out on the floor to stage a fall and called the paramedics, as this would increase the probability of encountering the right kind of physician in a hospital setting. The 911 operators, however, did not want to send Margie to the hospital that she requested; instead, they wanted to direct her to a hospital that was closer but also had a bad reputation for deadly staph infections that year.

At that point, it was difficult to even raise my arm, and I definitely couldn't get out of a chair. If I was lying in bed or fell down, there was no way I could get up. It gave me a great fear, being so helpless—like a turtle on my back. I started to keep a fire extinguisher near me in case I was alone and a fire broke out. Being so dependent suddenly made me very fearful. (M. DuBois, personal communication, February 3, 2019)

It's easy to run away from fear, but Margie did not run. Her fears may have been overwhelming, but her response to them was pragmatic. Instead of being overcome by her fears, she prepared herself as best she could, just as she did with her illness. Margie's attitude toward her fears inspires me and sums up her disposition as a whole: Instead of running away from fears, she faced them. Hope is an integral component of facing one's fears. All of us held out hope that she would be admitted to her preferred hospital, despite the obstacles before her. After calling repeatedly for nearly 8 hours, the 911 operators finally granted her access to that hospital.

Pay dirt: Margie had finally found the exact type of physician that she needed: a rheumatologist by the name of Dr. Goldberg. He took each of her symptoms seriously and recognized them almost immediately as dermatomyositis—a rare autoimmune disorder that is degenerative, incurable, and often fatal. Though Dr. Goldberg had only recently learned about this disease, all symptoms matched, and he decided to take immediate action in treating her. According to Santo et al., "death related to dermatomyositis...was more common among women" at a staggering mortality rate of over 70% (Santo, J. Souza, Pinheiro, D. Souza, & Sato, 2010, p. 600). It should also be noted that the mortality rate for women sharply increases after being 45 years old (Santo et al., 2010). Dermatomyositis also tends to be overlooked by doctors. Many patients often die before finding a proper treatment or a doctor with the right specialty. Given how advanced the disease was, my mother's chances of survival at this point were grim, but there was even more adversity to come.

Margie's new doctor started her on immunotherapy right away. She was given a strict regimen of a gamma globulin infusion every two weeks. Though experimental at the time, Dr. Goldberg convinced the insurance company that it could potentially be lifesaving. After two months of treatment, four treatments in total, the insurance company declined payment for her infusions, citing that it was experimental and should never have been approved. The insurance company sent my parents a bill for $64,000, which meant $16,000 per infusion. This was a major financial setback that my parents were entirely unprepared to pay. My parents' mortgage payment took up every last dollar that we had; there was no money left. Margie tearfully recounted,

> I called the insurance company to insist they cover my treatment. The lady on the phone was so snotty, assuming the doctor had just put me up to

it for research purposes. She didn't care about me. I wound up crying on the phone, pleading with her, "I can finally move again! Please don't take that away from me." (M. DuBois, personal communication, February 3, 2019)

It took two months without treatment and a letter from Dr. Goldberg for the insurance company to agree to the treatments once again. Due to the suspension of treatment, Margie's dermatomyositis had regressed, but she refused to give up. "I was finally feeling some relief, some control over my body. I couldn't afford to give up that chance of getting better" (M. DuBois, personal communication, February 3, 2019). Margie persisted through hope for regaining autonomy over her own body.

After resuming her gamma globulin treatments in October of 2003, Margie's breathing became difficult once again. "It was getting so bad, I was sitting still and could barely breathe. It was worse than ever before" (M. DuBois, personal communication, February 3, 2019). The nurse administering the infusion noticed her labored breathing and alerted doctors, immediately getting X-rays and bloodwork done. "They found lymph nodes on my lungs. I had cancer. There was so much of it in my chest that it pressed on my windpipe and wouldn't let me breathe" (M. DuBois, personal communication, February 3, 2019). Dr. Goldberg explained that dermatomyositis was often comorbid with cancer. Patients with dermatomyositis presenting "with lung cancer had a much worse outcome than counterparts without" this disease (Park et al., 2016, p. 384). However, those with "close medical monitoring...during longitudinal follow-up might lead to early detection of cancers and more prompt treatment, ultimately resulting in a better outcome" (Park et al., 2016, pp. 381–382). Had Margie not pursued her immunotherapy treatments so adamantly, there is a good chance that she would not have found out about the cancer until it was too late.

Though Margie's cancer had spread quickly, it was still too early to tell what type of cancer it was. Dr. Goldberg referred Margie to an oncologist at NSUH, who had her wait for the cancer to grow a little more so that they could target treatment appropriately. Though grief-stricken with the news, our family pulled together to support my mother. Our purpose was to get her through this and back on the path to health. "Waiting for the cancer to mature enough to figure out what kind I had terrified me, but I knew it was necessary" (M. DuBois, personal communication, February 3, 2019). My parents often put on a brave face for us, allowing my brother and me the space to grieve the news. We never gave up. Hope "consolidates the human will and creates a force that cannot be stopped in the consciousness of humanity. No adversary can triumph over hope" (Costa, as cited in Sieben, 2018, p. 85). As we prepared for her treatment, my brother and I would openly cry while whispering words of comfort and encouragement to my mother. Often my parents would cry too, the uncertainty overwhelming. This humanized my parents in a way my brother and I had never seen before, and it created a strong bond between us that still endures to this day.

Based on cancer's pattern of behavior, Dr. Donnelly determined Margie had Stage IV large B-cell non-Hodgkin lymphoma. Her treatment came in the form of an aggressive chemotherapy. The type used, however, caused my mother to experience cardiac arrest almost immediately. Due to many patients' weakened state, "heart failure...prevail[s] as the most common immediate [cause] of death" in those with dermatomyositis (Santo et al., 2010, p. 608). My father, who had been working that day, rushed to her side at the hospital as doctors struggled to revive her. Based on her extremely weakened condition, no one believed it possible.

Impossibly, Margie was successfully resuscitated, but she viewed her cardiac arrest as a personal failure. She was adamant that the doctors try giving her another chemo treatment again, but Dr. Donnelly made her wait. My mother's seven subsequent treatments went smoothly, but the cancer did not fully dissipate. Dr. Donnelly introduced Margie to Dr. Bayer, who would be the one to monitor the next steps of her treatment: a bone marrow transplant. This form of treatment was more harrowing than any treatment before: She would undergo a painful biopsy to learn that her stem cells—located in her bone marrow—were indeed viable and that she could donate to herself. "I remember asking for honey in my tea, but they wouldn't give it to me because it was too dangerous for my immune system—just like with babies" (M. DuBois, personal communication, February 3, 2019). This also meant that she would need to spend over a month in an isolation unit to insure recovery, as her new immune system would be equivalent to that of an infant.

Though the thought of undergoing a stem cell transplant and spending her recovery time in an isolation unit for an extended period was daunting, the hope of survival kept her going. "Hope is what keeps people motivated in life; and most importantly, hope gives us purpose" (Costa, as cited in Sieben, 2018, p. 84). My mother's sheer will to live gave us purpose, and the hope of seeing us as a family reunited gave her hope as well. When we were finally allowed to visit her, we had to decontaminate ourselves in an antechamber room and wear hazmat suits over our clothes to ensure we did not introduce anything that could threaten Margie's health. All of her antibodies had been eliminated with the bone marrow transplant. Though everyone was careful around her, she contracted a serious bout of shingles that encompassed the entirety of her back. "I had trouble getting comfortable, no matter what position I was in. It was just so painful" (M. DuBois, personal communication, February 3, 2019). No matter how much pain she was in, she was always excited to see visitors; though, we could not come as often as we would have liked. Between the strict visitation guidelines for bone marrow patients and the terrible ice storms that year, it was hard to visit. We spoke on the phone regularly, but the separation was difficult for all of us. Margie was the glue that held all of us together.

I struggled with depression throughout all of my mother's treatments, but with her away, I began to shut down. It was too much to bear. In her absence, I was severely depressed and had trouble connecting with the people in my life. Nothing felt real anymore. Though she had not died, the possibility that she *could* die was an ever-present and very real threat. As her primary caregiver, I would wake up worried that she needed me, but I was powerless to help her. This, I have come to understand, was unresolved grief, which can appear as "a cumulative restriction on our aliveness. Life becomes something to endure; the world seems like a hostile place to live" (James & Friedman, 2009, p. 57). I no longer had any interest in school or friends. I could not feign joy. Instead, I felt a constant state of numbness and fear, unless I was physically with my mother; talking with her on the phone helped, but to a lesser degree. All that I wanted to do was protect her, but all that I had left was the hope that she would be able to come home.

After her stay in the isolation chamber, Margie was sent to a special nursing home for another two months for physical therapy.

Hope is what kept me going. It ranged from simple things, like getting out of a chair on my own or having the strength to brush my own teeth, to having normal skin again that wasn't purple, bubbling up, and oozing clear liquid like a reaction to poison ivy. Some of my bigger hopes were to see you get married, to see your brother get married—just to see each of you smile with joy again. I needed to live in the hope that I would get to see that again. (M. DuBois, personal communication, February 3, 2019)

As we could now visit her more often, Margie's health markedly improved. She was eventually able to come home under strict guidelines for her immune system.

It was hope that afforded Margie the agency to push through dermatomyositis, cancer, cardiac arrest, and a bone marrow transplant, and to come out on the other side. Margie's tenacity for hope was both courageous and contagious—she kept the family strong in the face of adversity. When she was well enough, she decided to donate some of her time visiting patients in the hospital who were about to undergo their own bone marrow transplants. She wanted to give them hope for survival by letting them know they were not alone. Margie will be celebrating her 16th *re-birthday* this year and never misses an event coordinated by Dr. Bayer to support other bone marrow transplant survivors because, "I want to give others the hope for survival too, no matter what it is they are going through" (M. DuBois, personal communication, February 3, 2019). While she did not emerge unscathed—her illness and subsequent treatments have left her with severe neuropathy in both her feet and legs, teeth that break easily and often result in dental surgery, debilitating knee pain, and frail bones with a spongy texture that render many pain therapies entirely ineffective—she is unwaveringly happy to be alive. She is proud to share each moment that she has with us and with those who need a spark of hope to survive.

I later learned that, as dermatomyositis is still a very rare disease, there is not yet enough known about it to discern whether or not it is hereditary. No matter the outcome, I will approach it with hope and an "armed love" for my family, just as my mother did before me (Freire, 2005). "Statistical trends reveal that people with high life hope show up more, demonstrate more productively, develop stronger well-being, enjoy good health, and live longer" (Sieben, 2018, p. 73). Much like Margie's, my hope may very well determine my own ability to overcome serious adversity, such as dermatomyositis.

DISCUSSION

This experience with my mother's illness taught me that hope is a very real and viable mindset giving one purpose, agency, and meaning in life. As an educator, I am mindful to model hope for my students in the face of adversity, just as my mother has modeled hope for me. I make a point to make each student feel included, creating a space where they each feel heard and valued. "Students need to know someone cares for them as persons" (Noddings, 2005, p. 23). This occasionally means taking a student aside to check-in with them, especially if their recent behavior has changed. In my experience as a teacher, I have had students confide in me on numerous life events, including the serious illness of a parent, incidents of cyber-bullying, fears of coming out to their parents as gay or transgender, depression, and homelessness. I am sure to make them aware that I will get involved when I deem it necessary, and include authorities as needed—Most students whom I have encountered need to feel heard in order to develop a sense of hope.

When students have a sense of hopelessness, it is difficult for them to learn. I make it a point to find where the hopelessness is coming from and to find ways to rekindle that hope within them. "As teachers, if we maintain growth mindsets about building hope with our students, then we can work with our students to develop their hope levels, no matter what their hope starting points are" (Sieben, 2018, p. 74). Hopelessness, when addressed with sincerity and kindness, can be restructured and built back into hope.

Recently, I had a male high school senior confide in me that he always hated English class because he felt he was "too stupid" to understand any of the concepts for analysis. It made him hate reading altogether. When I asked him where this was coming from, he indicated that previous teachers had made him feel inadequate by singling him out when he didn't understand something in class. This happened with such frequency that it resulted in him shutting down in class entirely, developing a sense of deeply ingrained hopelessness and an expected trajectory of failure—not only in English class, but in all aspects of life. This student believed that he was worthless. As educators, we must be mindful to build students up by using their strengths, instead of tearing them down with their deficits (Sieben, 2018). Teachers need to be aware that, just as we are able to elicit hope within students, we are equally capable of stamping it out. "According to positivity expert, Barbara Friedrickson (2009), for every negative comment a person hears, it takes three positive comments to counteract the negative psychological effect it can have on a person's psyche" (Sieben, 2018, p. 81). My student's sense of failure was deep-rooted and pervasive. He needed a way to channel his sense of worthlessness into a sense of possessing value. After learning about his interests, I pointed out that his uncanny ability to fix machinery without instruction was a desirable skill, and that he might benefit from exploring where it could lead. He later decided to become a mechanic and had a great sense of pride. Students, especially those with such an ingrained sense of hopelessness, need us as role models for hope, both inside and outside of the classroom.

Interestingly, this student asked some of the most intelligent questions and brought up excellent discussion points about *The Kite Runner*, the novel that we were reading in class. When I inquired as to what spurred all of this, since he hated English class so much, he responded that "even though this is a difficult text to get through, I'm excited to read it. I've never liked a book before, but for the first time I actually look forward to discussing a book in class" (anonymous student, November 27, 2018). While I would love to take credit for his newfound ability to perform in the classroom, it was his newly rekindled sense of hope that permitted him to feel that he could understand the text and discuss it with confidence.

When I first met this student, I noticed that he would often try to get the class off-topic. I made a point to connect with him, learning about his interests and bringing them into class discussions. Eventually, he became more engaged with class texts and less interested in distracting others. Teachers must "create a supportive classroom community that promises to break down the hopelessness and build up the hope that is needed for life and school success" (Sieben, 2018, p. 81). As students began to realize that I showed an interest in this student, many responded by wanting me to get to know them as well, bonding us further and creating a space where all students felt heard and valued—both of which are vital to the empowerment of the minds of young adults. I am proud to have been a part of that experience for and with students, and to have had the chance to see how a little spark of hope could catch like wildfire.

It is my hope that as an educator, I can model and share this growth mindset toward hope with my students, to enable each of them to tap into their own inner strength to find meaning and purpose in life. There is a direct correlation between hope and academic achievement, and ultimately between self-worth and success. "Hope, taught in the classroom context of a school setting, can be raised" (Snyder, 2002, p. 262), and therefore, it is imperative that all students learn to cultivate hope as "a positive motivational state that is based on an interactively derived sense of successful (a) agency (goal-directed energy) and (b) pathways (planning to meet goals)" in order to thrive (Masten, as cited in Sünbül & Çekici, 2018, p. 300). If students can successfully learn hope strategies in the classroom, they can take these strategies with them throughout life, maintaining hope in the face of adversity. As I have learned firsthand, hope may be the only tool that a person has to survive adversity.

REFERENCES

Freire, P. (2005). *Teachers as cultural workers: Letters to those who dare to teach* (Expanded ed.). Boulder, CO: Westview Press.

James, J. W., & Friedman, R. (2009). *The grief recovery handbook: The action program for moving beyond death, divorce, and other losses, including health career and faith* (20th anniversary expanded ed.). New York, NY: HarperCollins.

Noddings, N. (2005). *The challenge to care in schools: An alternative approach to education* (2nd ed.). New York, NY: Teachers College Press.

Park, J. K., Yang, J. A., Ahn, E. Y., Chang, S. H., Song, Y. W., Curtis, J. R., & Lee, E. B. (2016). Survival rates of cancer patients with and without rheumatic disease: A retrospective cohort analysis. *BMC Cancer, 16,* 381–389.

Santo, A. H., Souza, J. M. P., Pinheiro, C. E., Souza, D. C. C., & Sato, E. (2010). Trends in dermatomyositis- and polymyositis-related mortality in the state of São Paulo, Brazil, 1985–2007: Multiple cause-of-death analysis. *BMC Public Health, 10*(1), 597–610.

Sieben, N. (2018). *Writing hope strategies for writing success in secondary schools: A strengths-based approach to teaching writing.* Leiden, The Netherlands: Brill | Sense Publishers.

Snyder, C. R. (2002). Hope theory: Rainbows of the mind. *Psychological Inquiry, 13*(4), 249–275.

Sünbül, Z. A., & Çekici, F. (2018). Hope as a unique agent of resilience in socioeconomically disadvantaged students. *International Journal of Evaluation and Research, 7*(4), 299–303.

Trüeb, R. M. (2001). Dermatomyositis. *Dermatologic Therapy, 14,* 70–80.

PART V

Conclusion

CHAPTER 17

The Importance of Narratives in Finding Hope in Grief

Stephanie Anne Shelton and Nicole Sieben

While losing both our fathers in the same year was a source of world-upending grief, it also extended our friendship profoundly. We had been friends before, but our losses connected us in new, and ultimately generative, ways. We also found ourselves in the contradictions that are higher education's efforts to support and dismiss such losses. We found ourselves sorting through sympathy cards while being reminded of professional obligations. We each had unquestionably supportive peers and students, but we simultaneously learned that higher education was not a space equipped to support grief in substantive and meaningful ways.

Stephanie sent an e-mail to her department as she sat in her car crying, preparing for the drive home to help plan a funeral: "I'm going to need to cancel classes this week. My father just died, and I'm headed home

S. A. Shelton (✉)
The University of Alabama, Tuscaloosa, AL, USA
e-mail: sashelton@ua.edu

N. Sieben
SUNY Old Westbury, Old Westbury, NY, USA
e-mail: siebenn@oldwestbury.edu

© The Author(s) 2020
S. A. Shelton and N. Sieben (eds.),
Narratives of Hope and Grief in Higher Education,
https://doi.org/10.1007/978-3-030-42556-2_17

to be with family and manage arrangements." She received two e-mails, one immediately following the other, from her supervisors. The first: "We are so sorry for your loss. Please share funeral arrangements when able, as we want to send flowers." The second: "We are so sorry to hear this news. However, the Graduate School requires that we account for missed hours, so please send alternative lesson plans as soon as possible." These two responses encompassed grief in higher education: genuine sympathy tempered by professional responsibilities.

Starting a newly acquired, tenure-track position not even a month after her father's passing, Nicole began the academic year teaching five new courses and coordinating the graduate programs in English education. These job-related responsibilities provided fulfilling mental stimulation, but they also left no time for personal reflection or meaningful grieving. In the early days of her position, an unanswered e-mail or closed office door could mean inattentiveness, and this was not a misrepresentation that a new faculty member could risk. Luckily, while the academic systems in place did not support healing, the kindness of colleagues sharing stories of their own journeys of grief helped Nicole to find comfort in community.

As researchers, our initial inclination was to understand how other scholars had experienced and discussed grief in the academy. What we found was unsurprising but disheartening. Discussions of grief were either framed within psychological and emotional literature or in self-help books. Neither applied. We were not looking to situate our personal losses within purely scholastic discourse, nor were we wanting someone to offer easy, but universal and therefore unhelpful, solutions. We simply wanted to know that we were not alone. We had one another, and that was something for which we were and remain grateful. However, when at conferences and other academic events, it was clear that many were unsure of how to approach us, of how to talk with us, of how to express their sympathy without awkwardly crossing personal lines. All while many of them were also processing their own forms of grief.

This book insists on erasing the formalities and the separating lines of academia in order to humanize grief as a real, ever-present, and important aspect of higher education. Here, 15 authors have offered pieces of themselves in an effort to assure the reader that not only are they not alone, but that they are *seen*, that they are *understood*. Because it is through acknowledging grief, in its many forms, that each author and we were able to find our forms of hope. Sometimes that hope is fleeting; sometimes that hope is life-changing. In all cases, that hope is an essential part of beginning to heal. This book is both a process of grieving and a product of our hopes. It has been in the planning stages for several years now, and its existence makes that hope real and lasting. And most importantly, this book makes hope something that the authors and we may share, in hopes that higher education might be more fully humanized, and for those reading, that your grief might be humanized and your hope realized. With collective hope, our efforts toward healing can be magnified, as the stories we tell each other and ourselves are all part of the quest for understanding and the persistence of hope amidst our grieving.

While grieving sometimes makes us feel closer to our lost loved ones, hoping makes us feel closer to ourselves. Hope can be a promise to persist in our skin despite our heartbreaks, to continue our personal quests for living and working and being, rather than trying to grieve and heal as others think that we should. When we hope, we travel pathways that are uniquely ours, though we may borrow strategies from others who have journeyed the roads of grief before us, and we share stories that follow suit. The beautiful narratives in this collection help us to witness other academics' pain, purpose, power, and persistence. In a graceful dance of grieving and hoping simultaneously, the authors write from authentic spaces to share their stories and to companion with us in ours. The stories show that to live *with* hope is not to live *without* grief. Rather, to live with hope is to live *despite* grief, or *because of* grief, or *alongside* grief. Our hope, much like our grief, makes us who we are as academics and as humans being in the world.

INDEX

© The Editor(s) (if applicable) and The Author(s), under exclusive   223
license to Springer Nature Switzerland AG 2020
S. A. Shelton and N. Sieben (eds.),
Narratives of Hope and Grief in Higher Education,
https://doi.org/10.1007/978-3-030-42556-2

Made in the USA
Columbia, SC
31 July 2023